ISLAMIC CLASSICS FOR YOUNG ADULTS

ATTAR

STORIES FOR YOUNG ADULTS

TRANSLATED AND ADAPTED FROM THE PERSIAN BY

MUHAMMAD NUR ABDUS SALAM

ILLUSTRATIONS BY
ROSE GHAJAR BAKHTIAR

ABC INTERNATIONAL GROUP, INC.

Library of Congress Cataloging-in-Publication Data
A catalog for this book is available from the Library of Congress

Attar, Shaykh Farid al-Din Abu Hamid Muhammad translated by Muhammad Nur Abdus Salam, Ph.D.
1. Islam—Young Adults 2. Islamic Literature
I. Shaykh Farid al-Din Abu Hamid Muhammad Attar II. Muhammad Nur Abdus Salam, Ph.D. III. Rose Ghajar Bakhtiar IV. Title

ISBN: 1-930637-06-3

Printed in the United States of America

Cover Design by Liaquat Ali

Published by
ABC International Group, Inc.

Distributed by
KAZI Publications, Inc.
3023 W. Belmont Avenue
Chicago IL 60618
Tel: 7732-267-7001; FAX: 773-267-7002
email: info@kazi.org/www.kazi.org

CONTENTS

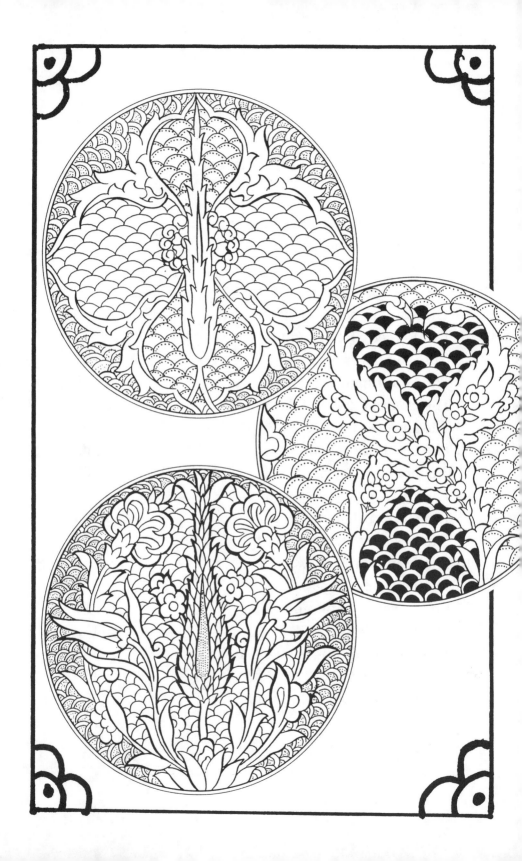

A FEW WORDS ABOUT ATTAR

Shaykh Farid al-Din Abu Hamid Muhammad was born in Kadkan, a town near Nishapur in the province of Khorasan, in modern Iran, but at that time part of the Seljuk Empire. Widely different dates are given for the year of his birth, but 1136 C.E. is probably as good as any. All accounts agree that he lived a long life, but the date of his death is also variously given. At the present time, scholars seem to think it occurred about 1230 C.E., making him about ninety-four, a ripe old age. His active life preceded that of Saadi and Rumi although both were born in his lifetime.

Farid al-Din's father was a perfumer, that is, a maker and seller of perfumes, and he followed his father in that profession. The word for 'perfumer' in Persian and Arabic is 'Attar,' and that is the pen name (*talakhkhus*) Farid al-Din chose for himself when he began to write poetry. Persian poets have always used pen names when composing their poetry, and they still do today.

But Attar was no ordinary poet. He was another of the giants of Persian verse. In addition, he was a leader of the mystical school of poets and was himself renowned for his knowledge and wisdom.

In those days perfumers were often doctors and pharmacists, compounding medicines and herbs for the health and welfare of the people. Attar is said to have been accomplished in medicine as well as the art of preparing scents.

It is reported that he left this employment and began to travel. He made a pilgrimage to Makkah and became a disciple of the famous Shaykh Majd al-Din Baghdadi.

Back in Nishapur, he devoted himself to Sufism and the mystic path to knowledge of God. He wrote many important books, mostly in verse, but some also in prose. Among the most famous are *Mantiq-al-Tayr* (The Parliament of Birds), *Musibat-namah* (The Book of Hardship) and *Ilahi-namah* (The Divine Book) from which the stories in this volume are drawn.

It should be noted that Jesus appears in two of these stories (stories 2 and 19). In classical Islamic literature Jesus often appears as world-traveler, walking from place to place. He observes and comments upon the things he sees and encounters, and occasionally intervenes. It is in this way that Attar depicts him in these two stories.

The same events, the Mongol invasions of the 13th century, which drove Rumi and his family out of Balkh to seek shelter thousands of miles to the west in Anatolia, caught up with Attar in Nishapur. Some reports say that he was killed by the Mongols during an assault on his home city. If that is true, it is a sad end for a man who devoted himself to the love of mankind and God. May God give him his just reward!

This translation and adaptation of Attar's stories is based upon the Persian prose adaptation from verse by Mehdi Azar-Yazdi.

Now let us journey back eight centuries to the world of

Attar and medieval Persia in these pages. Peace!

Muhammad Nur Abdus Salam, Ph. D.

1

RARE AND PRECIOUS

One day Sultan Mahmud of Ghazna, accompanied by his army commanders, went to the desert to hunt. They made their camp and set up the royal tent beside a green, tree-covered hill that commanded a wide few of the countryside.

While the servants were busy preparing lunch, soldiers were posted to watch the approaching roads and the commanders and princes, at the command of the sultan, went to hunt. Sultan Mahmud himself mounted his horse and went in search of prey among the hills and depressions of the wilderness. Spying a wild ass, he spurred his horse and galloped after it, becoming separated from his entourage as he did.

Riding up behind a hill, he suddenly met up with an old man who was struggling to replace a bundle of thorny branches that had fallen from the back of his donkey. The old man wanted to use the dead branches as firewood. No matter how much he tried, he was unable to put it on the donkey and was frustrated at his lack of success.

"Father," said Sultan Mahmud, "do you wish me to help you?"

Said the old man struggling with the bundle, "What could be better? I'll be able to put the load on the donkey's back and you won't lose anything. There is no one else to be found in this place to help me. You seem to be a well-behaved young man and doing good would not be unexpected from you."

Sultan Mahmud got off his horse and, while helping the man replace his load of brush on the donkey, asked: "Were you out here working by yourself in this desert?"

"Yes," the old man replied. "I don't have anyone to help me."

A little puzzled, Mahmud continued: "Then, how did you get this heavy load on the donkey's back by yourself the first time if you can't do it now?"

"I do this every day," explained the old man. "I thought about this problem in the beginning. I collect the brush on a hill and tie it into bundles. Then I dig a hole at the base of the hill. I put the donkey in the hole and then carefully, slowly put it on his back. Unfortunately, my donkey stumbled on a stone here and the load fell off. On this level ground there was no way I could put the load back on."

"Yes," reflected the sultan. "The works of man are thus! First we plan with care, but sometimes accidents occur."

Relieved that his difficulty had been solved, the old man became more talkative.

"Accidents are part of the plan. We don't know the reason for such things, but that One who should know, knows. Perhaps the load fell off to give you some benefit; I mean, the spiritual reward (thawab) of giving aid. Helping the helpless has much spiritual reward."

"Exactly!" exclaimed the sultan. "May God bless you, old timer! You have strong faith!"

When they had put the load back on the donkey's back successfully, the old man said: "I was very tired, but God is the Great Provider. If you hadn't come along, young man, I don't know how I would have loaded the donkey! Go now, so that God may grant you happiness!"

The old man's words delighted the king. After the old man had made the finally adjustments to the ropes holding the donkey's burden, Mahmud watched man and animal start out on the road. Suddenly he was seized with the urge to demonstrate his own greatness to the old man and to tease him a little. He rode back to his soldiers with all speed and said:

"Over there an old man is going with a donkey loaded with firewood. Go and block all roads to him so that he must pass before my royal tent!"

The soldiers hastened to block the roads as the sultan had ordered. When the old man reached one of the road blocks, the soldiers told him that he could not pass that way. "The road is closed and no traffic is permitted on it. Go by a different road!"

The old man said nothing and set off in another direction. He had not proceeded very far when a soldier stood in his path and signaled him to stop.

"You cannot go this way," said the soldier. "The road is closed and travel on it forbidden."

So the old man changed his direction again and chose another path, but the same happened again and again. The old man began to lose his patience. "What's going on today?" he demanded. "All the roads are closed! Where should I go?"

The soldier at the last encounter pointed in the direction of the sultan's tent. "That way is open," he said. "Don't you want to go to the city? Well, that's the way. You may even get there faster."

"They make the road longer and say it may be shorter," grumbled the old man under his breath. Then he smiled. "But, well, perhaps it may be shorter and I may get there sooner. Who knows?"

The old man led his donkey in the direction the soldier had shown him. After traveling a little while he saw some horsemen. There seemed to be some sort of commotion, but since he didn't have a quarrel with anyone, he paid no attention and continued on his way. The way led him inevitably in front of the royal tent. Around it there was a crowd of splendidly outfitted men on fine horses and soldiers with polished armor and weapons.

"What cruel soldiers!" the old man thought to himself, "making me and my skinny donkey walk among all those splendid horsemen!"

As he advanced further he suddenly saw the sultan's tent and he began to feel frightened. But there was no help for it; there was no other way to the city. He had to go that way!

When he neared the tent, he saw Sultan Mahmud sitting beneath a large, finely embroidered parasol on a throne. He was surprised to see that the appearance of the sultan seemed familiar in some way. Then he understood that the man on the throne who had helped him reload his donkey was a very powerful man, and not just that, but Sultan Mahmud himself!

"Just see who it was that I turned into a porter!" the embarrassed old man said to himself, lowering his eyes with shame as he approached the king.

When he was directly in front of the king the old man

greeted the king with "Peace," but in his embarrassment did not have the courage to look at Mahmud directly.

Sultan Mahmud replied to the greeting and asked: "Tell me, old man, what are you doing in this wilderness?"

"I beseech you, by God, do not shame me further," said the old man. "You know very well what I do. I gather brush in the desert and load it and take it to the city to sell. That is how I live, and I thank God for my livelihood."

"Well," said the sultan, "Since your collect firewood and sell it, why don't you sell it here?"

"Why wouldn't I sell it," asked the old man, "but where is the customer?"

That was what he said, but in his mind he added:

"He himself is certainly the customer. He has money, he has the mood. He helped me there and he won't stop until he was exasperated me."

"If you are selling the firewood," said the sultan, "I'll buy it."

"I know that you have no use for firewood here," sighed the old man, " but if you wish, I'll give it to you."

"I said that I wish to buy it," insisted Sultan Mahmud. "Tell me the price and take your money."

"All right," said the old man. "The price of the firewood is a thousand pieces of gold!"

One of the army commanders present roared: "A thousand pieces of gold! Are you mad? Is firewood so rare and precious in this desert?"

"No, sir," replied the old man. "Firewood is neither rare nor costly in this desert. But such a good customer is rare and a king is precious!"

Sultan Mahmud was delighted with the old man's response.

"If that is the way it is, I shall buy this load of firewood for two thousand pieces of gold!"

The money was given to the old man who wanted to leave, but Sultan Mahmud invited him to share the midday meal with him. After the lunch was over and old man was saying farewell, the commander said to him:

"Well done! You're pretty shrewd! With a pleasing word you sold your thorns at quite a price! And that in a place which is filled with thorns and brush!"

"It's too bad I needed the money," grinned the old man, "so I had to sell it cheap. Those thorny twigs are different from all the others in this desert. I've been gathering brushwood for forty years and I never came across a twig that had been touched by the hand of Sultan Mahmud. I really shouldn't have sold the load for less than ten thousand!"

Sultan Mahmud heard this exchange and was even more delighted with the old man's words. He ordered that the firewood gathered be given the remainder of the ten thousand pieces of gold.

"The price of well-spoken words is greater even than this," observed the king.

The army commanders were also filled with admiration at the ready wit of the old man and they each gave him a present.

And the old man, pleased and happy, went home with a bag of gold.

2
Dazzling, White Teeth

One day Jesus was traveling with several companions and came to a place where the body of a dead dog lay by the roadside.

Jesus stood contemplating the dead dog and then said to his companions: "What do you think about this?"

They looked at each other not understanding what Jesus meant. Then one answered: "It's the corpse of a dog which has died."

"What an unpleasant smell!" exclaimed another.

"It's a very disturbing sight," observed another of the companions.

"How dirty it is!" said another.

"Don't touch it!" warned another man. "You might catch some sickness from it."

"When it was alive, being a dog, it's body was unclean," said another. "And now that it is dead. . ."

"Look!" said another of the companions. "It's mouth is still open. "It's as though it still wants to bite someone's leg!"

Then Jesus spoke to them:

"What you say is true, but it was a faithful animal. It guarded well and could distinguish friend from foe. And how beautiful are it's dazzling, white teeth!"

You shouldn't see only the ugliness and the unpleasant. Whatever you encounter, you should look for its goodness and beauty.

3

THE BOY FISHERMAN

Once there was a poor black boy who had several smaller brothers and sisters. His father had died and his mother could do little more than the housework. So this boy, who was the eldest of the children in his family, had to spend his days fishing at the seaside. In that way he provided for himself and his family.

The boy was intelligent and clever, but he had no time to play. He had to spend his days on the shore trying to catch as many fish as he could.

There were other children there, too, but they were playing games together, so he would go off and fish at some distance from them. He would cast his small net into the sea and wait for the fish. While waiting, he would sit still sadly and fall into thought. Every day he hoped that today he would catch a lot of fish so that he wouldn't have to work the next day.

But the fish were always few and there was nothing left over for the next day. He had to provide for himself, his mother, and his six brothers and sisters. A family of eight had a lot of expenses. His found his only pleasure in the knowledge that he was supporting the family and his mother and his brothers and sisters respected him as the man of the household.

And that was the way it was when one day Sultan Mahmud of Ghaznah accompanied by his royal entourage happened to visit the beach to enjoy the sea. After taking his rest in a palace on the shore, swimming in the breaking waves and taking care of some other matters, the king suddenly felt bored. He had his horse saddled and rode off along the shore by himself to refresh himself.

The air was good and the sea calm. Along the shore people were busy with their tasks and pleasures. Groups of children were playing and laughing. Fishermen were going about their business. Some people were in the water enjoying the sea, others were lying on the sand in the sun or under umbrellas. Villagers, men and women, were working in the fields that were near the shore.

Sultan Mahmud rode on looking and observing all these things until he reached the spot, far from other people, where the boy sat by himself fishing. He was alone and paid attention to nothing except his own work.

The hooves of the horse on the soft sand made no sound. The sultan drew closer to the boy and then stopped to watch the boy who was completely absorbed in what he was doing and was amusing himself by reciting some verses his soft voice:

"I have a heart like a bird with a broken wing,
Like a boat stranded on the shore;
Everyone says: 'Tahir, play the guitar!'
As soon as it was plucked, the strings broke."

Sultan Mahmud realized that the boy was unhappy. He was affected by the boy's mood and wanted to console him.

"Dear boy," he said in a gentle voice, "what are you doing in this lonely place all by yourself?"

The boy looked up slowly and saw a man whose dress and fine horse told him that he was someone of importance in the land. The boy greeted the stranger politely and answered the question.

"I'm fishing," the lad said. "This what I always do. I can never play the way the others do. I'm different from them."

In these words the boy revealed his own unhappiness, that he was different from the other children, that he always had to work, that he had no time for play. . . .

"Well," said the sultan, "it doesn't cost anything to play. A person can even play by himself."

"But I have to provide food for seven others," the boy replied. "My mother, and my six brothers and sisters who are all younger than I am. You see, my father was a fisherman and he drowned in the sea."

"I see," said the sultan. "So how many fish do you catch every day?"

"One day less, another day more," said the boy. "Enough so that we don't all starve to death. We don't want to beg or be a burden on others."

"Splendid! Bravo!" exclaimed the sultan. "You are really quite a man despite your few years!"

He fell into thought, trying to find some pretext to help the boy without offending him. Then he asked:

"Are you ready to try something? Today I'll help you in your fishing. We shall be partners in whatever we catch."

"I agree," said the boy, "but on condition that we divide

the catch fairly. Don't expect to take a bigger share."

"I agree," smiled the sultan. "You shall have two shares, and I one."

"No," said the boy shaking his head vigorously. "I don't mean that. Senseless generosity always leads to trouble. I never take anything from anyone without a good reason. Half for you and half for me. God is generous, too!"

The boy's unselfishness pleased the sultan and he agreed to the terms. He tethered his horse to a stone and prepared himself to assist the boy.

"All right," said Sultan Mahmud. "If there are any fish in the net now, they are yours. Let's pull in the net and the start our partnership.

They hauled in the little net. It was empty.

"Very good," said the ruler, "but I don't think there are many fish in this place. Over there, where the water is a little deeper, there are likely to be more fish."

He took the net from the boy and cast it further out and into deeper water. He gave the rope to the boy and told him to sit right there. Then, after throwing a handful of sand into the water, he sat by the boy to wait for the fish and to chat. He asked the boy about his life and asked him to recite whatever poetry he knew and tell him whatever stories he knew. Then the sultan himself told some amusing stories and was pleased that the boy smiled and seemed to forget his sorrow.

After a while the sultan suggested that they haul in the net to see how many fish they had caught.

The net was filled with fish flapping about! The boy cried excitedly: "By God! Hundreds! thousands! I've never caught so many fish in my lifetime. There were always just one a few or none at all. You must be a very lucky person. This good fortune is due to you."

"No, my dear lad," said the sultan shaking his head. "It was your good fortune. It had nothing to do with chance of luck. We cast the net farther out where the fish are more plentiful."

"Okay," said the boy. "Now we must divide the fish. One for you, one for me, one for you, one for me, until they are finished. I don't want more than my share. God bless you."

"No," said the sultan firmly. "When we become partners with anyone, it is every other day. I didn't come here to fish, I just came to get some fresh air. The net was yours. You had selected the spot. So the today all of the fish are yours. When we work tomorrow, the catch will be mine. Is there anything wrong with this arrangement? This is not senseless generosity."

"All right," said the boy somewhat doubtfully, "but take two or three fish for yourself."

"No, thanks," said the sultan. "I don't want to upset the balance.'

"I agree," said the boy looking at all the fish. "These are enough to feed my family for several days. Tomorrow, then, we will definitely be partners."

"Definitely, definitely," said the sultan. "I must go now. God is great! Until tomorrow, then. We'll meet in the same place. May God watch over you!"

Leaving the happy boy, Sultan Mahmud rode off to his palace. For his part the boy went to tell the local fishmonger to come and take the fish.

When he reached the shore, the astonished man stared at the catch.

"You had a good catch today!" he exclaimed.

"Yes," declared the boy proudly. "I became the partner of a very good man today. They say that working with another person makes better work. However, today all the fish are mine. Tomorrow I won't get any fish. Whatever we catch tomorrow will be his."

The next morning Sultan Mahmud went to the seaside palace at the same time. He summoned a retainer and told him to go to such-and-such a spot on the shore where he would find a boy fishing. "Tell him that his partner of yesterday is waiting for him. Then bring him to me here."

The sultan's messenger delivered the message. The boy was frightened, but when he understood that his partner the day before had been Sultan Mahmud, he thought: "We don't have anything for anyone to take from us. And he wasn't a bad partner yesterday."

So he agreed, collected his net, and went with the retainer until they came to the palace.

The boy thought that they would go fishing again, but the sultan was pleased at the coming of the boy and said:

"Wasn't it agreed that yesterday we were partners and today we are partners. Yesterday I helped you catch fish, and today you shall help me in the work I do. Is there anything wrong with that?"

"No," said the boy thoughtfully. "We agreed that we would be partners today, but yesterday your good luck helped me. I'm afraid that today my bad luck will spoil your work. You know that I am not lucky."

"No," said the sultan. "Luck has nothing to do with it. There is a difference between work and thought. If I were to catch fish with a small net as you do, it would be of no account. If you were in a different line of work, you would be doing that. Look, these are my friends. Isn't that one black? Look at that one. Ten years ago he was a prisoner of war. Today he is an army commander. My own father was the slave of one of the princes. Whatever job a person happens to do, he can make progress according to his own ability and pains. In this world, all things are the same, and everyone has a job to do. Anyway, we made an agreement and today we are partners. And we have work to do that is more necessary than fishing."

"You are right," said the boy. "Now, what should I do?"

"Nothing," said the sultan. "You must sit here in the court and we will consult about whatever comes up and issue orders."

"All right," said the boy, grinning. "Today nothing will be decided or order without my permission! That is our agreement."

Upon hearing those words, the courtiers laughed and one of the sultan's companions said:

"Observe, your highness, this child doesn't deserve such affection. He's taking the thing seriously. Let's hope he doesn't cause any problems."

"He won't cause any difficulties," replied the sultan. "I take my promise even more seriously than he does."

So that day every matter that came before the sultan was resolved with the aid and counsel of the boy fisherman. There were a lot of things. One item concerned a huge mosque which the sultan wished to build on a large piece of land. In one corner of the land, however, an old woman had her house and she would not agree to sell it. It was her house and she was not ready to sell it at any price.

She had come to the court that day and they wanted to settle the affair. Smiling indulgently, they asked the boy what should be done.

The boy's brow furrowed in thought. Then he spoke:

"If the purpose of building the mosque is spiritual reward (*thawab*), then the old woman cannot be forced to sell house for the mosque. You have to either build the mosque some place else or make the old lady a partner in the mosque and name that part the 'Mosque of the Old Woman.' Just the way we are partners, your majesty. What's wrong with that?"

"If the old woman agrees," declared the sultan, "there is nothing wrong with that."

"That has always been my hope from God," she said.

The affair was settled in exactly that way and the young boy was delighted.

Next, news arrived that the governor of Khorasan had rebelled against Sultan Mahmud. The rebel had gathered an army and proclaimed himself king. He also intended to attack the sultan's capital, Ghaznah.

The sultan turned his young partner: "What do you say? How should we handle this matter? What should we do?"

The boy shook his head uncertainly. "By God, sir, I don't know. You have a good job, but it has a lot of problems. I think maybe it would be better if we made peace."

"That would be very difficult," said the sultan. "It is not such a simple matter. Peace is good when both sides are serious and there is no envy or greed between them. But when someone says 'Everything is mine!' there can be no peace. Yesterday, if I had wanted to take a couple of fish from you, would you have agreed?"

"Certainly!" smiled the boy.

"But suppose I wanted to take all of the fish. then what?"

"No," he said thoughtfully, "that wouldn't have been right."

"This affair is the same as that," said the sultan. "When threats and force are used, it must be stopped."

"You know better than I do," said the boy, "but couldn't we let him have Khorasan and live in peace? Just the way we divided the fish catch."

"That also cannot be," said the sultan. "Why? Because he was the governor of Khorasan and it was his duty to govern Khorasan on our behalf. Even though he hasn't taken all of Khorasan for himself, he is already preparing to attack our capital of Ghaznah! If he can get away with Khorasan, he will be greedy for other territory. If we give him Khorasan, tomorrow he'll want Balkh, and the day after Iraq, and then Tabaristan! If we do not oppose him, he'll take everything! There will be turmoil and violence and the peoples of this land will suffer. If that is the case, what is Sultan Mahmud for?"

"You mean what are we two for," reminded the boy.

The men of the court laughed. "Do you see that you yourself, who are nothing yet, will also suffer?"

"No," said the lad. "I really understand that the matter is very complicated. I can't think of anything else. Maybe it's better if we capture him and hang him."

"No, don't be too hasty," cautioned Sultan Mahmud. "It isn't that simple. After all, he isn't in chains before us now. Look, dear boy, he's one person who wants Khorasan and

other things. But if he were alone he wouldn't think about attacking Ghaznah. That means he has troops who will support him. That has made him bold."

The sultan paused a moment while he considered the situation. Then he said:

"Yes, but his supporters don't want to take Khorasan. Perhaps they have seen something in the governor that makes them follow him. First, let us see what quality he has that causes people to follow him. Is he just? Is he a good orator? Do people love him? Are they afraid of him? Is there some trickery involved, or is it something else? We must first learn this and then increase that quality in ourselves.

"Then, we must stop him. If he surrenders and repents, we shall forgive him, but if he fights, we must fight and destroy him. All of these things need a lot of planning and thought. It takes knowledge, it takes equipment, and it takes the cooperation of the people. Now, where should we start?"

"What you say is right," said the boy. "Giving in is sometimes like tyranny. But all of this is very difficult. It's not easy like fishing. I don't know anything about such matters. If I were alone, I wouldn't know what to do. It's a good thing that I have you as my partner!"

Sultan Mahmud and his ministers laughed. The commanders agreed that the boy was indeed very smart and a lover of justice.

So the sultan issued the necessary instructions and that day he settled a number of affairs, with the help of the boy. When the shadows were long and the day coming to an end, the boy fisherman said:

"My time is up. I don't work after the sun sets. My

mother and my brothers and sisters are waiting for me now."

"Very well," said Sultan Mahmud with a smile. "Now, we have been partners yesterday and today, but the results of each day's work are quite different. We worked much harder today than yesterday, so you may go to the treasury and take as much money as you want. How much do you want?"

The boy shook his head. "I don't want anything. We had agreed that the result of one day's work would be mine and the other yours. But everything today was your doing and the wages must go to you. You wouldn't take two fish from me yesterday, now I won't take anything. It wouldn't be fair."

"No," said Sultan Mahmud, "it would be fair. Yesterday we worked two hours and today many more. In order to be fair, you should take a greater share. Take what you wish."

"If that's the way it is, I'll accept the equivalent of a netful of fish as overtime pay and we'll say that we went fishing twice. So, tomorrow I'll play."

So they agreed and they brought in a lot of fish for the boy. Then the boy said: "So, the day after tomorrow will be a work day. If you want to be partners, you're welcome."

"You can see," said the sultan, "that I have a lot of work here. I must devote myself to these matters. If you wish, come every day and we can be partners here."

"No," said the boy. "I want to be by the sea. I made the partnership so that I could work by the sea. And you can't abandon all the work of the people, so let's say that partnership is over and the accounts settled."

"Very well," smiled the sultan. "But if you need anything, come to me."

"Thank you, sir," replied the boy, but if my net is full like it was yesterday, I won't need anything. I would be happy to see you but I like my work. My work is fishing and thanks to you I now know how to catch more fish. I have to go deeper into the water. . ."

So the boy said good-bye and took the fish he had been given to his house. But Sultan Mahmud privately appointed someone to watch over the little fisherman's family without the boy's knowledge. When the boy grew to manhood and still wanted to work on the sea, the sultan presented him with a boat.

4

THE WORSHIPPER OF GOD

One midnight Gabriel, who is the angel charged with delivering God's messages, heard God saying: "Yes, my servant!"

God was replying to the prayers of someone worshipping Him.

"It seems," said Gabriel to himself, "that one of God's pure and chaste servants is pouring his heart out to his Creator and that God is pleased with him. I can't ask anything about him at this time. It would be advisable for me to go and learn who this servant is and then come back."

Gabriel flapped his wings and flew through the sky and sought out all the places where God's faithful servants were, but he could not find this particular one. He quickly returned to his own place and saw that the servant was still praying to God and the God was listening to him.

"How is this possible?" Gabriel asked himself. "I am Gabriel and I don't know who this servant of God is? God may send me to him with some message or other and I must find out where he lives. I must go into the world and find him wherever he is so that I may know him!"

In the twinkling of an eye, Gabriel traveled to the earth

and visited the House of God at Makkah, then to Jerusalem, and other great mosques, but he could not find the person whom he sought. In this city, in that town, in the mountains, in the desert, in the islands, wherever there was a house of worship from among the followers of the great religions, he searched. He visited every place where at that time of night people were praying and confiding their problems to God, but he could not find the particular person he was looking for.

Astonished at this, there was nothing for Gabriel to do but return to heaven.

"O God!" he said at last, "You are the All-Knowing and All-Powerful. I wanted to find the person who was praying to You, but I wasn't able to do so. Who was that person who was so blessed that You listened to his prayers and took notice of him?"

God replied: "It would not be a bad thing for you to know him. Go to that large monastery near Rome so that I may make him known to you."

Gabriel flew to that place and saw that it was a temple containing idols. An idol-worshiper sat before a stone statue and called to the idol, weeping and sobbing loudly. He was praying and pleading. It was plain that he was very miserable and it was his voice that Gabriel had heard in heaven.

Gabriel returned to God.

"O God," he said. "I am Your obedient servant and do not know that which is hidden and I don't comprehend divine workings. I do not understand what is the secret here. Haven't we told people to worship the One True God? Haven't we sent all those prophets to the people to stop idolatry? So, I don't understand why You have been paying all that attention to that idolater!"

Gabriel heard the answer: "You do not know, but We know what We are doing. That man was not worshipping an idol, instead his heart was with Us. He is an simple person who does not yet know the way. All his life all that he has seen is that statue, yet he wants to be pure, he wants to be good. He wants to do good to others. He wishes well for other people and he does not give trouble to God's creatures.

"His heart is clean and his hands are clean. Everyone is pleased with him. Since he does not know anything except idol-worship, he thinks he must address the idol when he wants to pray and pour out his feelings to God. His heart is with the One who knows how to give him relief and lighten his heart. The statue cannot do that. It is We Who are God the Merciful, the Compassionate. It is We Who listen to the cries of the people when they speak the truth and want to serve. The voices of the prophets have not yet reached that man. If they had, he, too, would be a worshipper of the One God.

"Now, tell me, Gabriel. Who is there to answer his prayers if We do not listen to them?"

Said Gabriel: "No one. O Lord, greatness befits You! You know all things and the universe is established by Your kindness. All are in need of Your love and You are merciful to all."

5

THE REMEDY FOR BEGGING

Once in the city of Abarqu in the heart of Iran there was a beggar whose name fit his calling: Beggar Ali. He had gotten used to begging and no longer made any effort to work.

Why had he become a beggar? Indeed, that was the question, for when he was a boy of ten he had been an apprentice to a blacksmith and he earned ten coppers a day for his work, not much money even in those days. Then he was called "Master Ali."

One day Master Ali was sent with a jug to fetch some water. On the way he dropped the jug and broke it. Master Ali was afraid that if he returned to the shop empty-handed, the blacksmith would scold him. So he sat down at that very place and began to cry.

An old man passing by gave him a copper coin, saying: "Don't cry, lad."

"But, sir," protested Ali, "I'm not a beggar. The jug belonged to the blacksmith, my boss."

"That's all right," replied the old man with a smile. "Take the coin and buy a new jug. The blacksmith won't scold you. A new jug will cost just one copper."

The old man having given Master Ali the coin went on his way. The boy remained sitting staring at the broken jug, thinking what he should do when an old woman came and noticed the boy sitting by the broken jug. She also gave him a copper. She told him to stop crying and buy a new jug.

Now the boy had money for two jugs! While he was still marveling at this turn of events, another person stopped by the boy and gave him still another copper coin and some bread to boot!

More people passed by the boy, many of them stopping to give him small coins. . . .

Ali's eyes were opened. "I work in the blacksmith's shop from dawn to dusk and all I earn is ten coppers, but by sitting here for half an hour I've earned twenty! And I don't have to endure the blacksmith's rough words and abuse!"

When it was noon and the boy was still sitting there, a woman came out of her house nearby and saw the boy and the broken jug. She went back in and came out again bringing a jug very much like the one that lay in pieces in front of him. Giving it to him, she said:

"Stand up! Take this jug and fill it with water and finish your errand. There's no point in just sitting here."

"But I'm late," whimpered Ali. "My boss will beat me."

"I'll go with you and urge him to forgive you."

So the woman went with Master Ali to the smithy.

"Sir," she said to him. "The lad's not at fault. The cistern was crowded and a lot of jugs were smashed. Don't blame him this time. He'll be more careful next time."

"All right," said the blacksmith and the woman left. When he was alone with the boy, the man turned to him and frowned.

"Look, boy, when you broke the jug, you should have hurried right back to tell me instead of saying bad things about me to people. I don't want an apprentice who brings dishonor on me. Here, take these ten coppers for today's work and be off with you! If you weren't a beggar by nature, you wouldn't have taken money and things from people!"

Ali didn't know what to say. The twenty coins were still in his pocket. He left the shop slowly and went into the street. Then he stopped to consider the situation.

"First I'll go and clean up the pieces of the broken jug," he said to himself. "I don't want the street in front of that kind woman's house to look messy."

He went there and collected the pieces of the broken jug. Then he thought that if he went home early, his step-mother would quarrel with him and scold him. So he went to another street, laid the pieces at the foot of a wall and sat beside them.

"Before I decide whether to go home, I'd better look for an omen," Ali said to himself.

He drew lines in the dirt. "I'll call this one 'good' and this one 'bad.' If it comes out 'good,' I'll go home; if not, I won't."

Ali made his calculations and saw that the omen was bad.

"So, I must stay here and see what happens," he told himself.

A man came up to him.

"Whose jug was that?" he asked pointing to the pieces beside Ali.

"My boss', the blacksmith's," Ali replied. "I went to fetch some water and broke it."

The man pressed a coin upon the lad. "Here, take this and buy a new jug." Then he went on his way murmuring these verse:

> "A lad broke a jug and wept:
> 'I don't dare go back;
> What can I do if the blacksmith asks me?
> The jug was his, not mine!
> Breaking the jug has broken my heart;
> The work of days is nothing but breakage!
> If he blames me, asking about the jug,
> I have nothing to say on my own behalf. . .'"

*****

When evening came, Master Ali returned home, but he said nothing about breaking the jug and losing his job because he was afraid of his stepmother. The next morning he went to the place where the pieces of the broken jug lay. . ., and gradually he got used to being a beggar. That is, the people made him a beggar. No one tried to earn spiritual reward (*thawab*) by making him learning anything to increase his self-esteem. However, they continued to shower coins on him to gain a reward from God for themselves. In this way they spoiled him and made him into a beggar.

A person will employ his brains to advance in whatever line of work he chooses or into which he falls. One person works in industry and makes new things. And another improves his skills is the art of begging! So the youthful jug-breaker gradually learned how to appear poorer and more miserable in order to gain more sympathy. And more coins.

Every day he devised some new way to appear more wretched. One day he pretended his hand was paralyzed. Another day he dragged his foot as though he were lame. He rubbed dirt on his clothes. He pretended to faint. . .With these and other devices he got the people to give him more and more money. It is not strange, therefore, that he no longer tried to do any work. People seemed to want it that way.

Time passed and Master Ali grew up to be a man called Beggar Ali. After so many years of pursuing his calling in his own city, Beggar Ali started to think about travel. So he set out, from village to village and city to city.

*****

Now in those days Nishapur (in the northeastern region of modern Iran) was a great city, as famous as Baghdad and Balkh. And so, begging as he traveled, Beggar Ali came to one of the gates of Nishapur.

A soldier on guard at the gate narrowed his eyes and looked at him.

"Who are you? What is your business? Where do you come from? How much money do you have?"

"I am called Beggar Ali," said Beggar Ali simply, "and I come from Abarqu on the other side of the great desert. I am poor and miserable, but I have a little money."

"Do you any trade?" demanded the guard.

"Of course. I know a little smithery."

"Good," said the guard, relaxing his manner somewhat. "You may enter, but mind that you don't beg in Nishapur! The citizens don't want beggars here and don't give money to them."

"Certainly," said Beggar Ali, but in his heart he did not believe the soldier's words. As he walked along a street he spied a bakery. Extending his hand, he said in a whining voice: "May God lengthen your life. In God's way, give this poor person some bread."

"May God lengthen your life, too," replied the baker. "My prayer is for your prayer, but it is obvious that you are a stranger and don't know that begging is illegal in Nishapur."

"What does 'illegal' mean?" asked Beggar Ali with surprise. "When someone is hungry what should he do?"

"If someone is hungry," said the baker, "he should go the local public kitchen. They'll give him something to eat."

Ali got the directions to the public kitchen from the baker and went there.

"I'm a stranger here," he said to the staff at the public kitchen. "I don't have anything to eat."

They searched Beggar Ali and questioned him. "You say you don't have anything to eat, but you have this money. Use your money to get food and then go to local workhouse and they'll give you work to do. No one in this city gives anyone bread for nothing. This public kitchen is for persons who don't have a single coin!"

"Suppose someone is sick and can't work," rejoined Beggar Ali.

"The he must go to the local hospital and be treated. If he can't be treated successfully, then they will send him to the local jail."

This news astonished Beggar Ali, but then he recovered and said to himself: "This is nonsense. I'll go and beg as usual."

During the next few days he roamed about the city and spent all of his money. He tried to beg, but no one would give him any money. When he uttered prayers for someone's well-being, instead of a coin, the reply would be: "If you know any prayers, then pray for yourself. We also know prayers: 'May God give you life!' 'May God help you!' 'God have mercy on your father and mother!'"

When he tried: "It's Friday Eve," or "It's the eve of the first of the month," someone might answer back: "The eve of the first of the month to the eve of the last of the month! It's all the same! Night is night. Friday Eve is not yours to sell; it belongs to everyone. Friday itself is for those who work six days a week."

Ali would reply with a curse. The man from whom Ali had hoped to get a coin would retort: "We know curses too, but they are a kind of nuisance. Creating a nuisance can get you a fine here!"

If Ali pleaded that he was hungry, they would direct him to the public kitchen. If he said he was sick, he would be shown the hospital. If he said that he was out of a job, he would given the address of the workhouse.

Beggar Ali employed every trick he knew to get sympathy and pity, but still no one gave him even the smallest coin.

Finally, one day he saw another beggar in a street. Ali was delighted to find a comrade in the trade, so to say, in Nishapur.

"Brother!" exclaimed Beggar Ali going up to the man. "How do you survive in this city? I can't get anything out of these people!"

The Nishapuri beggar answered: "The people of this place are charitable to those who work. If someone gives alms to someone for no just purpose, he'll be fined by the governor. Begging is illegal here; and so is giving to beggars or encouraging them."

Ali was perplexed by this answer. "But, then, why are you a beggar?"

"I'm not a beggar," said the Nishapuri straightening his shoulders. "I'm an employee of the Public Inspectorate. My job is to dress up like a beggar and roam about to see if anyone will violate the law and give me money. If someone does, I arrest him and take him to the court to fine him for encouraging begging and beggars!"

"What an absurd, nonsensical city this place is!" declared Beggar Ali. "What do the people do when they want to give charity or alms? Are mercy and generosity now become sins?"

"No," said the Nishapuri shaking his head. "Mercy and generosity are very good, but here everyone who wishes to give alms and charity puts his money in the box for the needy. The money is collected and spent for those who must eat at the public kitchen or are in the poorhouse and are infirm or feeble. An able-bodied man must work. There is a workhouse in every quarter and work to be done is given those who are out of work."

"Thank you very much," said Beggar Ali. "It's plain that because of these arrangements, there is nothing to do except work. Begging won't bring any free bread."

"No, it won't," agreed the Nishapuri. "Unless it is not known."

Beggar Ali went on his way thinking about what he had learned. The next day he took a bucket and he thought to himself: "I'll carry this bucket with me and no one will know that I am a beggar. Then I can beg in some of the quieter streets where there aren't so many spies to see me. If someone tries to get me to empty his garden pool, I'll say that my foot hurts and pretend that I'm not able. In the end, people will feel sorry for me. The women are better than the men in that respect. Everything will be all right as soon as I start crying: 'Ladies! Ladies! For the good health of your children! I haven't eaten anything today. . .!'"

So Beggar Ali left the busy, crowded streets behind and entered the infrequented narrow lanes. At the beginning of a dead-end lane he called out: "Pool water! Pool water! I change pool water! I beat rugs! Pool water!"

When he reached the end of the lane he began to call out instead: "Ladies! Ladies! . . ."

Halfway down the lane, someone came out and said: "What's going on here? Why are you disturbing the people's peace? Don't you know that shouting in this place is illegal? It's a kind of public nuisance. If the inspector sees you, you'll be taken to court. Now, I'm a decent fellow and I don't like to bother anyone, but be careful and watch your step. Don't shout in the street! People are trying to rest in their homes."

Seizing the opportunity, Beggar Ali cried: "My good fellow! Since, by God, you are a good man, tell me what I should do. I'm a stranger here and don't know what I should do in this city. Is cleaning garden pools something bad? Is one permitted to sell soapwort?"

"Yes," replied the householder. "A person can buy and sell anything freely which is not harmful to people, but you cannot shout and hawk wares loudly in the streets of Nishapur. It is illegal. If you want to sell soapwort you must find a spot and then sell it quietly. Just as people have ears, they have eyes. If someone needs some soap-wort, he'll come to you where you are and buy it from you. If he doesn't want any, well, he won't be bothered by the shouting."

"As you say, sir," said Beggar Ali. "But tell me one thing, who takes care of the garden pools in this city?"

"A branch of the local office of works takes care of that. They send laborers to do it. In the same way they collect trash. There are shops to handle cleaning rugs. There are places to buy clothing and other things. There's no need to go about the streets shouting. That's old-fashioned."

Beggar Ali thought about this a moment. "But what do you do about old, dry bread? Do you throw it into the trash?"

"No, sir! We don't throw it into the trash. Everything is well-organized here. The dry bread is collected and once a week men from the local poultry raisers come and buy it. The money they pay is used for the needy. There is a box for money to be used by the needy in every street and lane. We don't return old bread to the baker so that he can mix it with fresh bread!"

"Excellent!" exclaimed Beggar Ali. "But what can a person like me do? I'm a stranger here and I don't have any food. I don't have money to pay for a room in an inn."

The man laughed at Ali's ignorance.

"The first day he eats at the public kitchen. The first night he sleeps in the public dormitory. The next day he works and has money. In short, there is no place for begging in this city. The reason is that the people do not want to turn others into beggars."

"I understand," said Beggar Ali. "They've thought of everything. Public kitchen, poultry coop, jail, poorhouse, inspectorate, workhouse, public dormitory, court. . . When people don't want to make more beggars and don't encourage begging, then everything is fine. But it was first the people who made me a beggar. I wasn't a beggar, I was a blacksmith's apprentice and my name was Master Ali. I wasn't Beggar Ali. People made me a beggar thinking only of their own spiritual reward (*thawab*). God punish them for that!"

*****

Beggar Ali had nothing left to pay for food. The next morning he went to the hospital and declared: "I am sick and I am poor."

He still did not want to work.

He was examined and told that he wasn't sick. "If you're poor, than go to the local work office."

He found himself with no other option, so he went to the local workhouse. They put a broom and a sieve in his hands and told to go to a certain street:

"Sweep the street and then separate the sweepings with the sieve. Put the dirt in the barrel and the other trash in the garbage can. When you've finished come back and take your money."

Beggar Ali went and did the work. He collected his money and for the first time after many years of begging tasted the delight of work and respect. The next day the work office sent him to clean the garden pools in two houses. The day after that he was sent to wash the stone walls of the Tomb of Shaykh Attar.

That night he told an acquaintance in the inn where he was staying that he had washed the walls of the tomb of some saint.

His companion shook his head.

"That wasn't a saint's tomb. It was the Tomb of Shaykh Attar, the very man who people say was a dervish and a recluse. But he worked more than anyone else. He was a pharmacist and he made the medicines that made many sick people well."

"Be that as it may," said Beggar Ali, "in that place I swore to myself that I shall never beg again. I don't want to be called Beggar Ali any more. I want to become Master Ali once again."

So, as time passed, Master Ali was no longer satisfied with these small jobs. He wanted to do something more important. One day he went to the chief of the local work office and told him that he knew smithery.

"Wonderful!" the other exclaimed. He sent Ali to the shop of a blacksmith that made horseshoes and Master Ali once again became a respected craftsman.

As it happened there was in that smithy a young boy serving as an apprentice. Whenever the boy was sent to fetch water, Ali would always tell him: "Dear boy, be careful not to break the jug. But if you do, don't get upset about it. A jug is not more important than you are. Just come back and I'll buy another one. And, if you break a jug, don't wait around the broken pieces. Collect them and throw them into the trash and run away from that place! Run away from it!"

"Master Ali," his fellow workmen would say, "you seem to worry about the jugs a lot."

Ali laughed. "I know something that makes me dislike breaking water jugs."

Ali continued to work in that smithy. Soon the other workmen were addressing him as "Craftsman (*ustad*) Ali."

Then one day he was sent with some of the others to the city of Sabzevar to shoe the city governor's horses.

In Sabzevar someone saw dressed in his work clothes and thought that Ali was a beggar. The man reached into his pocket and offered Ali a coin.

Master Craftsman Ali looked at the coin and then at the man.

"What's this?"

"Money," replied the good man. "Aren't you poor?"

"You're the poor man!" said Ali. "It's been a while since I was poor. I'm an honest workman and I live with honor and respect now. Do you want me to become a beggar again? It's too bad that you aren't in Nishapur so that I could take you to court and have you fined!"

"Fined? Why?" cried the man in amazement.

"Because," said Master Craftsman Ali firmly, "the people of Nishapur don't want to make other people into beggars. want to have And the governor of that city knows how to cure them of the habit!"

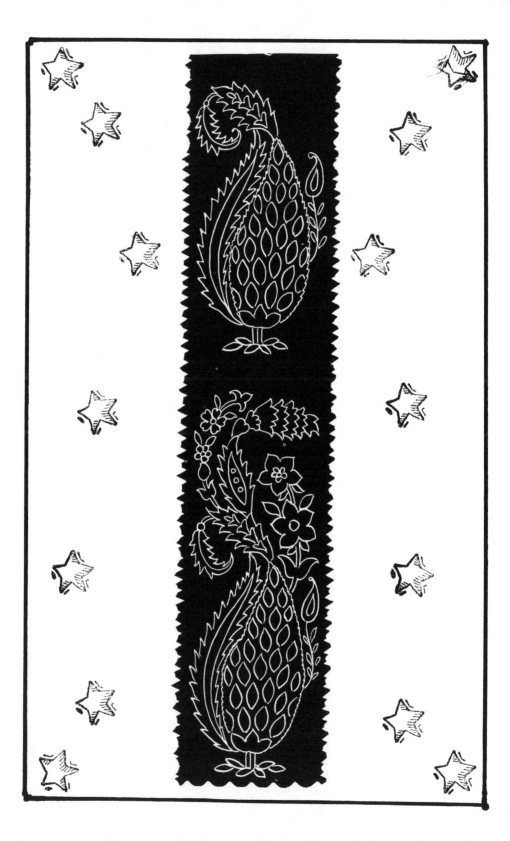

6
ONE, NOT TWO

Once long ago the governor of a certain city had a beautiful daughter who had many suitors. From time to time friends of the ruler would find some excuse to discuss weddings and marriage, taking the opportunity to mention some young man who, in the friend's opinion, was worthy, properly qualified, and desirous of taking the young lady as his bride. He would certainly be loving, true, and so forth.

However, they were afraid to formally propose marriage lest they be rejected, something that might sour relations between themselves and the ruler. They hoped that the governor take the hint and choose the bridegroom himself.

But the ruler understood this and never allowed the matter to be discussed further. And the girl had said: "I shall agree to marry someone only if he wants me for myself and not because I am the daughter of the governor."

Matters were thus when on one of the festival days all the friends and associates of the governor were assembled to celebrate. Eventually the question of the marriage of the governor's daughter came up again.

"I've heard a lot of talk about this, friends," said the governor, "but everything has its proper time. Today my daughter and I wish to discuss the matter seriously. We must choose one from among the suitors and we haven't the patience to discuss this at length. So let me say this:

"Tomorrow I shall betroth my daughter to whoever loves her the most. Therefore, whoever wishes to press his suit for her hand must come tomorrow morning so that I may tell him the conditions of marriage and for my daughter to see her prospective husband. We can sign the marriage contract and celebrate the wedding on the same day, that is, tomorrow!"

Amid much excitement, the people left the assembly to inform the lovers and suitors of their acquaintance that whoever desired to wed the governor's daughter must be present at the governor's palace in the morning so see what happened. "We don't know what the governor is planning," they would add worriedly. "We've never seen a marriage arranged in such a fashion, as though it were some sort of contest!"

But the next morning only three men showed up! The rest of the professed lovers were afraid that the governor might punish them for something so they forgot their love; their fear was a greater. And, too, there was the possibility of getting into trouble.

The governor received the three men in his audience chamber. After he had learned their identities, he summoned his daughter and said to them:

"It is clear that among all of the suitors for my daughter's hand, you three are more loving and truer. Now, here is my daughter that you may see her. If she agrees, we will complete the marriage ceremonies today. However, I am the governor of this city and marriage with my daughter has certain conditions."

The governor stood up.

"I shall now tell you the conditions," he continued. "I shall give you half an hour to write your opinion of it on a sheet of paper. Afterwards, my daughter and I shall decide in the way we think best and act accordingly."

He glanced at his daughter who nodded modestly, then continued:

"The conditions are these, that I tie each of my daughter's suitors to this pillar and beat him as much as I please. If he is still alive after that, he must live with my daughter wherever we say. They must live on his earnings, however small or great they may be. He must never enter my palace. He must never complain to me about anyone. He must never come to me for a favor. He must not hope for anything from me. If he behaves badly with my daughter and leaves her, I shall order that he be skinned alive!

"Furthermore, if any of you three, after coming here, does not agree to these conditions, he must leave the city within forty-eight hours and never return to it. He must never mention me or my daughter again. If he disobeys these commands, I shall know how to deal with him!"

The governor looked sternly into the eyes of each the three suitors. Then he went on:

"Now, here are the three sheets of paper. Write your replies within half an hour and sign them. In this way I shall know to whom I may give my daughter as wife."

Having said this, the put one of the sheets of paper in the hand of each man. Guards escorted each one to a separate chamber. Then the guards closed the doors and stood beside them.

When the half hour was over, the governor and his daughter returned to the hall. A justice and a mulla were with them carrying the marriage contracts.

"Bring me the papers," commanded the governor. The guards opened the doors and suitors were let out with their letters in hand.

One of the suitors presented his letter. The governor took it and said: "This is one."

The second suitor handed his letter to the governor.

"Two!" said the governor, placing it under the first letter.

The third suitor's letter went under the first two.

"Now we shall examine them in order," declared the governor.

The first suitor had written:

"Though it is very difficult for me to forget my love, in accordance with the command of Your Excellency I shall try to leave the city within forty-eight hours. I pray that Your Excellency not trouble any of my family or relatives, only I was a suitor from among them. No one else has any responsibility for my actions."

The governor and his daughter exchanged glances and smiled.

"Very well," the governor said. "The matter of the first suitor is settled. He is not a lover; rather, he is insincere. He wanted my daughter in order to be near me and he did not want to suffer any trouble for her hand. He does not know that a lover must endure many trials, just as a lover of knowledge and learning must take pains and work hard to become learned. A person who is not steadfast will abandon the difficult path halfway along and flee. This young man is cowardly and thoughtless, too, for he did not imagine that the problem had any other solution. He did not consider that perhaps our conditions were merely a kind test, or that we might be lenient with him.

"In any event, each person knows himself best. Therefore, we have nothing more to do with this one. He must leave and never look back. He will forget us and we shall forget him so that he may rest easy."

So the first suitor departed and it was the turn of the second.

He had written: "I accept all of the conditions for marriage and am prepared to do what is required. If I live after the beating, I shall achieve my desire. If I do not live, I shall weep for her in the next world. I don't want to live any other way. Death or the governor's daughter!"

After reading the letter, the governor turned to his daughter.

"What do you say, my dear?"

"I don't want a crazy husband," she declared.

"Bravo, my girl!" smiled the governor. "You have spoken well. This one is ready to be tied to a pillar, beaten, and afterwards live at our command like a slave and remain far away from me! He is willing to endure hunger and to fear me as though a sword were dangling over his head as long as he lives!"

He looked the second suitor in the eye.

"How is my daughter different from other girls?" asked the governor. "Why would you buy this love at such a miserable price?"

He turned to the others:

"I cannot be confident that this one is sane and in his right mind. He should go to a mental hospital and be treated there. Furthermore, there was nothing about my daughter in his letter! It was all about himself! He is not a true lover, rather he is mad. A mad son-in-law will not do!"

Shaking his head, he looked at the second suitor again. "Go quickly and forget us so that we may forget you and that you may be at peace."

And now it was the turn of the third suitor. He had written:

"I have a cousin who has no defects, but I love the governor's daughter more. I think we shall be happy together. I will not leave the city unless I am forced to do so, and that would be tyranny because I have offended no one. With respect to the other conditions, I also do not like the idea of being beaten and living in fear and apprehension in order to get married. Such a life would not even provide for the happiness of the bride.

"I am a lover and a suitor only if she too accepts me and the governor reduces the harsh terms of the conditions. If not, well, what is wrong with my uncle's daughter? I think that for every problem there is a third way to solve it. I pray that the governor will not be offended by my words as I have no quarrel with anyone. Rather, I want to take a wife and live peacefully. Whatever the outcome, I hope for the happiness of the governor's daughter."

The governor asked his daughter: "What do you say?"

The girl bowed her head modestly and said: "Whatever you command. No one else has come."

The governor laughed. "Very good! This young man is intelligent. He knows that there is no real difference between my daughter and the daughter of his uncle, but since he loves mine more, he thinks you both would live more happily together.

"This young man is intelligent because he neither fled from fear nor did he accept a beating out of madness. Rather, he found a third way.

"Know, young man," said the governor to the third suitor, "that my conditions were a test. I, too, have no quarrel with anyone. I, too, wish for the happiness of my daughter. Now the choice is yours. Are you ready to complete the marriage ceremonies right now and without any special conditions? If you are not, I hope that you will be happy with your cousin and we shall be present at your wedding top congratulate you. Now what do you say?"

"I came here with great hopes and desires," he said turning to the governor's daughter.

"I too," she said softly.

"And I," said the governor to the court in a strong voice, "with the greatest pleasure announce your betrothal. I pray that God may bless you and grant you both a long and happy life together!"

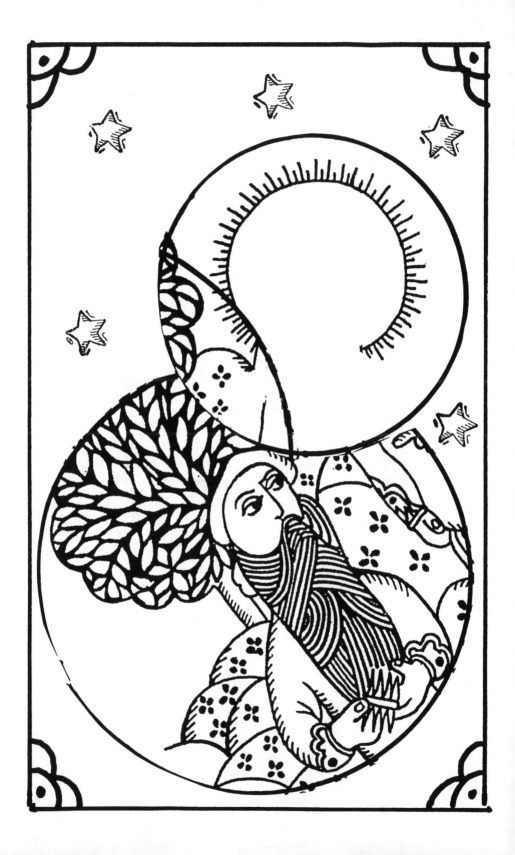

7

THE WORSHIPPER'S BEARD

During the time of Moses there lived a pious man, a devout worshipper of God. He lived apart from other people and spent his days and nights worshipping God. Nonetheless, the man knew that somehow, despite all of this worship and prayer, he had not achieved the spiritual state and satisfaction that he should have.

From time to time, while combing his thick, long beard, he would fall into thought and say to himself: "I don't understand what is wrong with what I am doing. I have no worldly goods. I have given my heart to God. So why don't I believe that my prayer and worship is pleasing to God?"

Things were thus until one day he visited the Prophet Moses and said to him: "O Moses, this is the way things are with me. I don't know why I don't enjoy all of this prayer and why I feel uneasy and don't believe in my own goodness. Please, when you go Mount Tur and pray to God, ask Him why I do not find any pleasure or state in what I do, why my tears don't flow, why my heart does not tremble from purity and ecstasy. I spend my days and nights in the worship of God, like all the friends of God. What is the reason for my failure?"

"Very well," said Moses. "I shall ask Him."

So when Moses was deep in prayer and private conversation with God, he asked about the unfulfilled worshipper and why he did not feel the fire of love.

A Voice called to Moses:

"Moses! It is true that this man you speak of has made himself in appearance like My pious worshippers. He prays day and night, but there is one thing missing, and that is sincerity. In any work, sincerity is the condition of perfection. The thoughts of a person must be sincere and entirely focussed on the object. Sincerity is not found just on mountains and in deserts, it is everywhere. There are many who live among men, but are completely with God. Sincerity gives purity and pleasure and brings delight and enthusiasm.

"But this man's heart is not entirely with God. There is always a part of it concerned with his beard. He is constantly combing his beard. When his forehead touches the ground in prostration, he wonders whether his beard is touching the ground, too. When a visitor comes to him, he wants to tidy up his beard. When he looks into a mirror he is more concerned with the appearance of his beard than he is in thanking Us for the eyes and power of sight We have given him.

"It is true that he praises God and offers many prayers and keeps apart from evil things, but his preoccupation with his beard has taken the place of other things.

"What is the difference if one person is thinking constantly about money, another about status, another about cheating and hypocrisy, and he about his beard?

"Since he is not sincere and his remembrance of God is not pure, his heart is not pleased with himself. His worship gives him no satisfaction. That is why he does not believe in his own purity and goodness, and he is right to do so."

When Moses came down from the mountain, he tried to explain this point to the man in every way he could:

"You must do something so that when you are worshipping God, you are not thinking about anything else. Look, brother, if you wanted to study something, you have to concentrate all your thoughts upon the subject. If your mind wanders to your clothing and appearance, you won't learn anything. If you want to enjoy a poem, or the view of a garden or field, you must concentrate your thoughts upon it. If you don't, you won't get any pleasure from those beautiful things. In short, you must forget about your beard. That is the source of your problem."

When he heard these words, the worshipper of God felt deeply ashamed of himself. He burst into tears and cried: "That's right. That's the way it is with me! I spend too much time thinking about my beard. When I am praying, my mind sometimes wanders to the way my beard is moving as I speak. This beard doesn't let me be sincere."

The man grew so upset that he began to pull at his beard and pluck out its hairs as he wept. He kept blaming the beard for his trouble: "I don't want this beard any more! I don't want it. . . ."

Moses was deeply affected by the man's regret and confusion. At that moment Gabriel descended from heaven and said to Moses: "Do you see, Moses? Now that he understands the beard is his problem, he still will not let it alone. Before he was always thinking about beautifying the beard; now all he is thinking about is pulling it out. The beard is not at fault. Thoughts must be sincere. Are there not many men with beards who are not always thinking about them, but thinking about their work and how do it successfully. But those who cannot help but think about beards, or clothing, or other such things will never taste the delight of ecstasy sincerity and purity."

8
THE SPARROW'S GREAT ADVENTURE

One day Solomon was passing through a wilderness with his army. In that region the birds were in the trees, busy with their own lives, and in one of the trees there was gathered a flock of sparrows. They were flitting from branch to branch and making a lot of noise with their chirping.

Among those sparrows there was a pair of lovers. They were perched on a branch and talking to each other.

The female sparrow said: "Look over there! That's King Solomon marching with his army!"

"Forget about King Solomon!" said the male testily. "Let's talk about ourselves."

The wind which was under the command of Solomon brought the voices of the birds to him. When he heard his own name mentioned, he listened carefully.

"No," the female was saying. "My point was just look at the splendor of Solomon and his retinue. What clothing! What horses! What a wonderful life they must have!"

"Better than our life?" demanded the male. "We're sitting here beside each other and no one knows how happy we are."

"Of course we're very happy," said the female sparrow, "but just think how many wonderful things there are in this world; how many good things. . ."

"Yes, there are many things," said the male, "but you are more beautiful than all of them, and we are better than all. When we're together we don't need anything else."

"That's true, of course," said the female. "We're very good, but there are great differences between people's lives. Why there are things we don't have. For example, we don't have King Solomon's famous Flying Carpet."

"Carpet?" demanded the male with some annoyance. "A carpet is just a heap of woven wool, and they have given it a name: King Solomon's Flying Carpet! What good is that, anyway? They sit on it and travel about and have to watch that they don't fall off! But we! All we have to do is beat our wings and fly lightly and easily wherever we want. Believe me, we are starting a good life together that no one else has. Come, let's fly up to that higher branch so that we can better enjoy the scenery of the desert."

So they flew up to a higher branch. Then the female said:

"You said that King Solomon's Carpet was nothing. But what does that huge army eat?"

"What does the army eat? Nothing. Just what we eat. We eat fresh grapes. They eat raisins, which are dried grapes. We eat fresh rice and wheat and the seeds of the fields eat, but they throw them into storehouses and eat them when they are spoiled."

"But, beloved," replied the female, "we still don't have everything. There are lots of other things. Sweet breads.

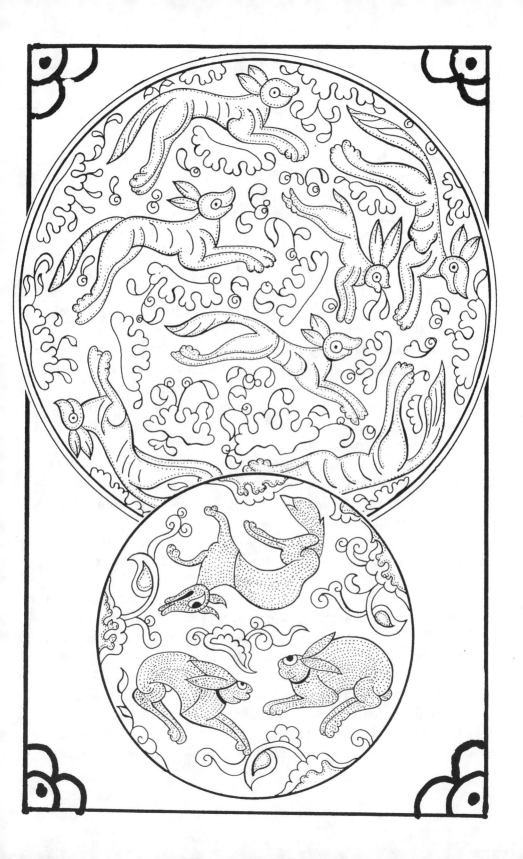

There is, I say, cheese. There are lots of other things. Didn't you see the peacock feathers on his cap? And that thing around his neck which sparkles so. . ."

"All right," said the male. "I'll get everything for you. Up till now we haven't missed anything. After this I'll get anything your sweet heart desires. We live much better than Solomon does. It's a good thing that King Solomon himself is my servant. If he gives me any trouble I'll knock down his great dome and his audience hall with one kick! They'll fall down in ruins on his head."

Then some other sparrows alighted on that branch and the two lovers stopped their conversation, but their remarks had reached the ears of King Solomon.

When Solomon returned to his palace he sat on his throne under the great archway and commanded that the sparrow be brought to him.

So they went and brought back the male sparrow. The sparrow greeted the king in peace and sat before him.

"What were those things you were saying about me?" asked the king.

The sparrow began to tremble in fear. "Your majesty," he answered, "I am very small. I wouldn't dare to do such a thing! I would give my life for you."

Solomon picked a hazelnut out of a box of nuts and threw on the floor near the sparrow.

"No," the king said. "You, who cannot break open this nut, how dare you claim to be able to bring down this dome and this hall around the head of King Solomon. My dear little fellow, bragging has limits. Boasting has a reckoning. Why do you utter such nonsense which insults us? If a frail sparrow such as you can dare to say such things, what may we expect from a lion, a leopard, or an elephant?

And what will people say? Didn't you stop to think that what you were saying was unreasonable?"

The sparrow saw that King Solomon's tone was rather fatherly. He began to feel safer, so he replied:

"Your majesty, you are in the right. I didn't mean anything by it. I wasn't giving a speech or leading an army. I was talking with my own fiancee. I love her very much and we want to get married. With such talk of adventure and daring deeds, I wanted to impress her with my importance and suitability. Love is always accompanied by jealousy. I wanted her to think that I was above everyone else. Everyone talks thus in private. I didn't want to be impertinent to your majesty. O God, what shall I do? What a fool I was to tell her those things."

King Solomon smiled at the despair of the small winged lover and said: "We forgive you your words this time. But always try to speak in a way that suits your condition so that in the future you may not be embarrassed."

9

THE INCENSE BURNER

Once there was a poor old woman. All she had in the world was a decaying old house, nothing else. She had no skills, so she lived by sitting in front of her house with an incense burner at her feet. She would burn wild rue in it and repeat to each passer-by: "Let the eye of the envious explode! Let the cleansing smoke blind the eye of your enemy!"

Now everyone knew how beneficial to health and fortune the smoke of wild rue was, so people would waft it over themselves and then give the old woman some small change. In this manner she was able to live.

The people of the neighborhood were so used to seeing her sitting in front of her house with the incense burner that they would give directions to strangers looking for a particular house in this way: "It's near the house of the old woman who burns incense." Or: "It's a hundred steps up the lane from the house of the incense burner." Or: "It's a few steps before you reach the house of the old woman who burns incense."

Now it happened that in a house near the house of the old woman there lived a rich man. He would see the old woman sitting behind her incense burner everyday and give her something from time to time.

But one day something happened.

The rich man bought some fresh pistachio nuts in the market and wanted to send the package to his house. He gave the seller his address, but the porter couldn't memorize it. The rich man tried to explain in several ways: "My house is in halfway down the street; it's on the left; its door is painted green; the number is 16; there is a paving of green stone in front of it. . ."

"I understand," said the porter finally with a knowing grin. "Next to the house of the old lady incense burner."

"Yes, that's right," said the rich man sharply. The porter left to deliver the package, but the rich man was upset at the porter's words.

"People know my fine house because it is next to the wretched hovel of a beggar, an incense burner!" he said to himself with annoyance. "That's not right. I am a respectable man, a man of substance. Yet whenever I want to give someone my address, it always comes down to 'it's next to the house of the old woman who burns incense!'

"They are right when they say that a rich person cannot be happy among a lot of poor people. So long as everyone is not fortunate, no one can find peace. I must do something about my neighbor."

After considering the problem for some time, the rich man decided to buy the old woman's house. "I'll clear the street free of her and her incense burner!"

That night when he went home he summoned a real estate agent and told him to offer to buy the old woman's house. The agent went to the woman and asked:

"How much do you want for your house? I have a

buyer."

"I'll never sell it," said the old woman firmly. "This house is all I have to remind of happier days. I will stay here until I die."

When the rich man was informed of her answer, he realized that he would have to adopt a different method to get the house. At the same time he knew that it would not be good for his reputation if the people knew he was determined to get the old woman's house.

"I'll ask her to see me," he thought to himself, "and stop her burning incense in the street. If she is needy, I'll provide for her. If she is determined to continue what she is doing. I'll do something else."

He told his servant to invite the old woman to his house.

When she came, the rich man greeted her and asked how she was. His wife and children were in the room with him.

She replied:

"I thank God Most High! Your children are very kind to me and I thank them for helping me."

Then the rich man turned the conversation to the business of burning incense. "What good does burning wild rue do?" he asked.

"Don't talk like that!" said the old woman. "For generations people have said that the smoke of the wild rue protects against the evil eye. Everyone knows that!"

"What does the 'evil eye' mean?"

"Why, it means the eye of envy and jealousy! When one person is jealous of another, he can't stand to see the other have any good fortune. If he has the evil eye, the moment his gaze falls on man or thing it will do its work! From that time on, misfortune will follow!"

The rich man laughed aloud. "What strange things I am hearing!" he said. "How can one glance of an envier destroy someone's life? Nothing is like that! Look, dear lady, when a building is made strong with brick and plaster, the evil eye cannot harm it. To tear down such a building you need picks and crowbars, or you must shoot a cannon ball at it."

"No, sir," insisted the old woman. "What I mean is that if the evil eye strikes something, in some fashion or other ruin will follow and the owner of the building will lose it."

"That's not so," said the rich man. "The owner loses the building only when he himself wishes to sell it, or, through some mistake of business, he becomes a debtor and is forced to sell it to raise money. But all of that has nothing to do with the evil eye! If the evil eye really worked, no one in this world would ever get rich because anyone who has more than others is envied. And why is that only the poor and the unfortunate concern themselves with the evil eye? Why don't we worry about it

The old woman shrugged. "That is up to God. Perhaps the rich do some good deeds which block the evil eye."

"Charity and good deeds are something else," said the rich man. "They do that because they feel they should. But it has nothing to do with the smoke of wild rue! If the wild rue is the remedy for everything, why should anyone give charity or do good deeds? All he would have to do is throw some wild rue on the coals and go to bed. The truth is that the wild rue smoke has nothing to do with good and bad. If it goes into your own eyes, they will hurt. Have you ever wondered why wild rue is supposed to fight the evil eye?"

"What do I know?" said the old woman spreading her

hands. "Perhaps it's because the smell is good."

"Not even that! A flower has a better smell. The smell of a rose is good. When you burn aloeswood and sandalwood, the smell is good."

"Well," said the woman in triumph, "aloeswood and sandalwood are expensive, but wild rue is cheap!"

The rich man was losing patience.

"Yes, but pomegranate and orange skins are cheaper! And they smell better!"

"But there is something else more important," retorted the old woman quickly. "When wild rue is burning, it cracks and explodes! Just the way it explodes the evil eye!"

"No," sighed the rich man. "A branch of wet firewood in a fire will crackle and snap even more loudly. Anyway, all seeds explode in a fire. Orange pips, nuts, gourd seeds, watermelon seeds—they all explode noisily when heated. Guns and cannons also make a lot of noise, but all that has nothing to do with the eyes. It has to do with the ears!"

At those words the rich man's wife and children burst into laughter. Even the old woman laughed.

"Sir!" she said. "You have a lot of patience. What do I know about such things? I don't know why wild rue is good. People have said it is for generations, that's all I know. So why do people always say that?"

"In the old days people used to say a lot of nonsensical things. Just because they believe something is no proof that it is true. In the old days people used to believe things about medicine and sickness that we now know were wrong. Wild rue first became useful because its smoke drove off mosquitoes and insects. Then gradually people began to add things about it and in time believe them."

"But, good sir," said the old woman, "now that you

know these things, I want to say something else. Personally I have no faith in wild rue. Several years ago my husband was sick and no matter how much wild rue I burned, it was of no use. Last year my son went to prison, and burning wild rue did not change anything. And look at me! I am the incense burner of this street and I am poorer than anyone else in the neighborhood. If it was beneficial, the incense burner should be better off than anyone else, but as you see, I am not.

"I know that burning incense is a kind of begging, but what else can I do? It's good for me that people believe me when I tell them that the smoke will protect them from the evil eye. They give me some coins. If not, I have no one to provide for me. I don't know how to do anything else. And my son can't help me."

The rich man was affected by her words.

"Well," he said seriously, "You yourself admit that wild rue smoke is useless. Now what can we do so that you don't have to burn incense in front of your house. It is bad for us. Does our being your neighbor harm you in any way?"

"Of course not, sir! I am very grateful for the help and aid you and your family give me. I always pray to God to bless you, but if you want to do something for me, arrange to get my son out of prison."

The rich man glanced at his wife and children and leaned forward.

"Why is your son in prison?" he asked her softly.

"For no reason!" answered the old woman heatedly. "He didn't do anything, good sir! He was just burning wild rue. He learned how to do it from me. From the time he was a child he saw me doing it. I used to walk about with the

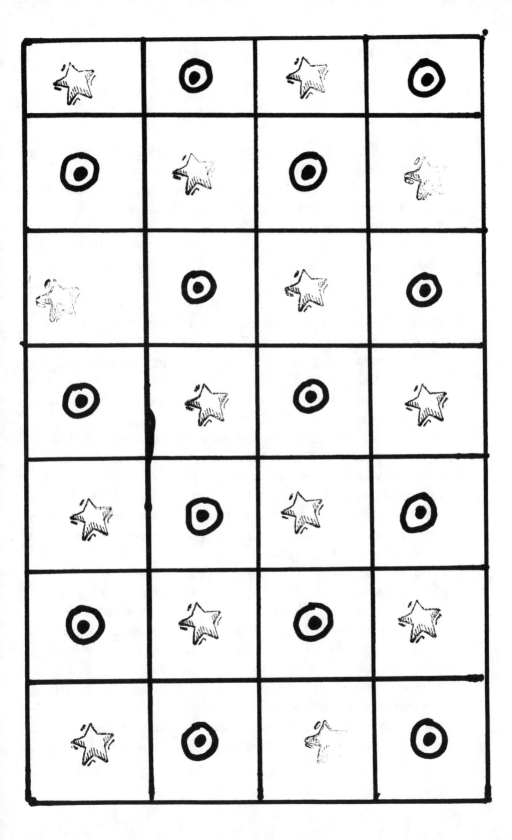

burning incense. He walked with me and when he got bigger he started to the same thing himself. Then last year he was in front of a butcher shop burning the incense and asking for money. The butcher didn't believe in it, like you, and he made fun of my son. My son said some bad things to him and a fight started. To make a sad story short, he was arrested for disturbing the peace and now he is still in prison."

Hah!" exclaimed the man. "Another miracle of the wild rue! Now, tell me, when he gets out of prison, will he go back to the same line of work?"

"If he finds a better job," said the old woman, "why should he? Do you think anyone wants to be an incense burner? It's no different from begging. No, perhaps it is worse, because it is a kind of fraud."

"Very well," declared the rich man. "Come here and live with my wife and children. If you do not want to do that, take what you and live in your own house. You are our neighbor and have the rights of a neighbor. I will look into the matter of your son and arrange to get him out of prison. But, the condition is that you don't burn incense in front of your house any more!"

The next day, he sent workers to repair the walls of the old woman's hose and paint it. The old woman was made more comfortable. Shortly afterwards, her son was released from prison. Her rich neighbor arranged a job for him and the mother and son began to have a decent and respectable life. Then she went to the real estate agent and offered her house for sale. The agent promptly reported the news to her neighbor.

"Why do you want to leave now?" he asked her. "We don't want to lose a good neighbor. Why do you want to move away from this street?"

"We are always grateful to you and pray for you," the old woman replied. "You have freed us from incense burning. We want to move because everyone here knows about our being incense burners and we want to go somewhere and live where we can have respect."

"It's good that you understand that," said the rich man. "I know that when a person thinks of the peace and comfort of his neighbor, he himself has peace and comfort. Now, first find a suitable house for us to buy, and then we will negotiate about this one."

10
THE OLD LUTE PLAYER

Once there was a man who knew no work except how to play the rebeck, an old instrument something like a lute, but played with a bow. He had learned this as a child in his home city. When he was a young man he played and sang at public and private parties, and received gifts of money for the pleasure he gave the people. He lived this way until he became an old man.

But in his old age, he was not as nimble on the rebeck and his performances no longer were so pleasing to the people. His invitations to perform at parties fell off. Day by day, he found less and less work. The people began to refer to him as "the old lute player." They called him that because they did not distinguish between a rebeck, played with a bow, and a lute, which is played by plucking with the fingers, like the guitar. Besides, the lute was a more famous instrument.

The old lute player, as he was called, now found himself living in the city of Nishapur, but it was not a good place for a musician to ply his trade. The people were very religious and strict and did not employ musicians at parties and gatherings except weddings. It wasn't possible to just play anywhere, in the streets or markets, in the hope of small change from passers-by. The people gave money to beggars, but not to musicians. They would say playing music was sinful.

So the old musician roamed about the streets playing his rebeck and once in a while his playing pleased some-one who would give him some small coins. In this way he managed to earn enough to keep himself from starving, but that was about all.

Now it happened that when the old man's fortunes were at their lowest ebb, the governor of the city was transferred and a new governor took over, stricter even that the previous man. He proclaimed that music was for weddings and the Eid festivals. Why should there be any playing of music in the streets on other days? People had more important things to do than to listen to idly to music. Playing music at other times was religiously unlawful (*haram*)!

After that, the old man had no way to feed himself. The people wouldn't listen to his rebeck, nor would they give him bread by way of alms. He used up what little he put aside, and one day found himself hungry and without any food or the means to buy it.

"Should I beg?" he asked himself.

He wasn't a beggar. He considered himself a musician and an artist. But his work no longer would support him and he knew no other trade.

"What kind of a skill was it that they had taught me?" the old man said to himself unhappily. He wept over his misfortune. His heart was broken and he didn't know what to do.

Concealing his rebeck under his robes, he went to the Grand Mosque of Nishapur. He didn't see anyone else in

the mosque at that time of day, and he thought that that was better. . . .

He went to the prayer niche (*mihrab*) and sat before it. Taking out his rebeck he placed his hand on it and raised his head to the heavens and began to speak to God Most High.

"O God! I know not what sin I have committed. I have never done evil to anyone. The people do not want me. There is none to think about my condition but You, who provide sustenance for all. You will not neglect me!

"O my God! I know no trade other than playing this rebeck. This is my own rebeck. This is the tool of my only skill, but these days I have no audience. So, come and be my audience. You know what I am saying. You know that I want to work. This is my job, but no one rewards me with bread for it. No one sings with my music. I have been driven out of every place. No one wants me and I won't play any more for these people.

"I am helpless and weak. I have no family. Because I have no one else, I am with You. From this time on, I shall play only for You. If I am not skillful enough for You, please forgive me. What else can I do? I have nothing else. It is good that the mosque is empty. If someone were to come, he would drive me out of Your house. . . ."

The old man, weeping miserably, began to play his rebeck. The playing made him feel better and as he played the words of some songs came back to him and he began to sing along with his music. Lost in his music, he paid no attention to what was around him. He didn't even know what he was doing. Playing the rebeck, and that in the *mihrab* of a mosque!

So the old man played and sang and wept. In the end,

he grew tired and fell asleep in the *mihrab*.

However, the mosque servant had heard the first notes of the old lute player and had gone into the enclosed part of the mosque (*shabestan*) and watched him playing and listened to his words. He sympathized with the old man and could not bring himself to give him more trouble and rebuke him. So he left the poor old man in peace and went straight to the retreat of the great saint Shaykh Abu Said.

Shaykh Abu Said was a man who had mastered all the knowledge of his age. He knew what the religious scholars said and what the Sufi mystics said. He had a hospice (*khaneqah*) where he taught his many followers. The people respected him greatly, but some of the religious scholars opposed him and said: "Abu Said is wrong. Instead of prayer he recites poetry, and instead of the Traditions of the Prophet, he talks about mystic knowledge."

Others, however, believed him to be a man of God and would say the Abu Said has realized Truth. In any event, the mosque's servant was a disciple of Abu Said.

When he was with Abu Said, after describing to him all that he had witnessed on the mosque, he said: "I don't know what I should do. It is very bad to play a musical instrument in the mosque, but I felt very sorry for the old man. I've come to you to see for advice."

"Stay where you are until I see what happens," said Abu Said. So the servant sat where he was while the shaykh taught. While this was going on, a man entered the room with a purse of money in his hand. He went to the shaykh and said: "O shaykh! I have sworn to give you the money in this purse, because through you I have been successful in something I wanted to do. Please give this to some needy person."

Having said this, he handed over the money and left.

The shaykh's disciples knew that some times the shaykh would give them a portion of the money and they hoped that this would be the case today.

But the shaykh gave the purse to the mosque servant and said: "This belongs to the old musician. He is more deserving than anyone else. Take it and give it to him, but do not tell him where it comes from. Tell him that these are the wages for the work he did for God and God has given it to him. It belongs to no one else but him. Tell him that whenever he has the need for more, he should go to the same place in the mosque and speak with God about it, but tell him that he should not play music in the mosque. Tell him to take his rebeck and go to the khaneqah of Abu Said. That is a dervish house and no one will bother him when he plays. A mosque is for prayer (*salat* or *namaz*)."

The mosque servant returned to the mosque and waited patiently until the old man woke up. He placed the money in front of the musician and repeated the message of the shaykh.

The old lute player was overcome with surprise at his good fortune. He prostrated himself in the *mihrab* and thanked God, saying: "O God Most High! You are a good God! You know the value of music better than any artist. I praise You and I shall not play for any other person except You."

The old man took the purse of money, put his rebeck under his robes, and started to leave without asking the mosque servant anything.

The servant, however, reminded him: "Dear father, don't forget that whenever you want, come here. Pray and pour out your heart to God, but don't bring the rebeck. Take the rebeck to the dervish house of Shaykh Abu Said and play it there."

The old man shot a reproaching glance at the mosque servant.

"Who is Shaykh Abu Said? If he is a man, let him leave his work and come here and play for God!"

Having said that, the old man left the open-mouthed mosque servant staring after him in astonishment.

11
BUSINESS AND LUCK

In the old days, people of one city often got news of the conditions in other cities very late. For this reason, merchants usually traveled about from city to city to get first-hand information they needed to conduct their businesses. On these journeys they would buy and sell goods, hoping for a profit.

Because of this, the supply of goods to the market was often late or arrived suddenly in large quantities resulting in a collapse of prices. People would say that a "camel-cat" (*shuturgurbah*) was at work in the market. Of course, there is no such thing as a camel-cat, and the phrase meant "contrary conditions" or "nonsense." In any event, no one was able to make sound predictions about the marketplace. That was because the people did not have enough information about what was going on in other places.

We know that in those times the highways between cities were not safe and secure. There were a lot of bandits and brigands who preyed upon lone travelers. People who had to travel tried to do so in large groups or caravans. Such a large group would have a better chance to fend off attacks by highwaymen.

Travel by sea was a little safer, but still there were pirates who attacked merchant vessels. And there was also the danger of a ship's sinking in a storm or when it struck rocks.

So, being a merchant was a difficult work. The merchant had to risk the loss of his capital; but, on the other hand, the profits could be very good. Whenever a task is more difficult or dangerous, the rewards are much greater. The world never stops its activity, so the merchants did their work like the rest of mankind.

*****

In this story we have to do with two merchants from the same city who traveled about by sea to conduct their businesses. Most of their experience was of trading in ports. In the days of sailing ships, such trading voyages could last months and even years.

On one of these trips, the two men had each bought a large quantity of goods and loaded on it on the ship. They met each other for the first time in one of the ship's cabins. They talked together and got to know each other. This done, it became known that one of them had bought a large amount of animal oil (butter and ghee) and the other a large number of copper utensils. With God's help they hoped to sell their goods at a profit and then buy things they thought might earn still another profit when they sold them upon their return. After all, that is what business is all about.

So the ship set sail and was at sea for several weeks. When they were in the middle of the sea they encountered a passenger vessel coming from the opposite direction. When the two ships reached each other, they came close and hauled in their sails.

As was the custom, the captains dropped sea anchors and then discussed the conditions of the sea and their ships. If one or the other needed something or had some problem, they would try to help each other.

While the ships were near each other and their captains visiting each other and exchanging news, the oil-merchant received permission to go into the other ship and walk about in the hope of finding some relative or friend aboard.

Now the oil-merchant was a sharp, calculating man, and he used every opportunity to get the latest prices and information about what was going on in the market. However, the copper-merchant paid no attention to such things. "Our job is to buy and sell goods," he would say. "What will happen will happen."

So the copper-merchant slept while the oil-merchant got in a small boat and was rowed to the other ship. Once aboard, he enquired about the conditions of the markets and prices of goods in the ports on the other side of the sea. He learned that the price of oil was very low, while, on the other hand, the price of copper was soaring!

Having learned this, he returned to his own ship. On the way he considered what he should do. He realized that when he sold his oil at the destination he would lose a lot of money. This upset him very much. When he returned to the cabin to share with the copper-merchant what he saw, his fellow merchant was still fast asleep.

When the copper-merchant finally woke up, the oil-merchant said to him: "It seems that we have met a ship carrying passengers from where we wish to go. Don't you want us to go above and look at it?"

"What's there to see?" asked the copper-merchant. "I don't know anyone in that ship."

"I feel the same way," said the crafty oil-merchant. "Everyone is going up to look at the ship, but I'm too tired to bother!"

But the oil-merchant was greatly distracted, thinking about the low price of oil in the market in which he was planning to sell it. Gradually his thoughts began to focus on a solution: if he could manage to exchange his oil for the copper of the copper-merchant, then all would be well.

When the ship was underway again, the oil-merchant opened the subject with the copper-merchant, saying: "Last year I sold my oil there and bought cloth to take home. I didn't do badly. What merchandise did you take last year?"

"I haven't been on this route for several years," said the copper-merchant. "The only goods I have now are the copper utensils. My business is always random and without calculation. Whatever happens is all right with me! I don't understand what I'm doing. Hah! Whenever I've tried to plan it all out, I've usually suffered losses. Now that I am on this trip, I have no idea what will happen. Whatever will be, will be!"

"Of course," agreed the oil-merchant affably. "A man must trust in God's goodness, but carelessness and a lack of planning do not work in business. Now, I didn't want to say anything before this, but you know that place we're traveling to has dozens of copper mines! In fact, it exports huge amounts of copper! That's why I think that your goods, well. . . God willing, I hope it will work out for you, but what do I know?"

Upon hearing this, the copper-merchant became a little uncomfortable. "No problem," he said with determination. "If the market for copper is bad, well, copper is a thing that can be kept for years and not spoil. It doesn't decrease in quantity, nor can it be eaten by moths or termites, or ruined by worms. It doesn't burn or rot. It's copper and it's always copper. There is only one difficulty; I can't stay there a long time until the market changes because I have to return home quickly."

"If that is the case," said the oil-merchant, "it would be right if you took my oil. As it happens, I intend to remain in that city for a long time in order to learn their language. If the copper market is poor, I could keep the copper until times were better and the price higher. But oil is something that must be sold quickly as it can spoil."

Said the copper-merchant: "Do you see? Things in this world are always thus! Reversed!"

The oil-merchant stroked his beard.

"Even though I got a lot of profit from selling my oil last year," he said slowly, "I'm willing to exchange my oil for your copper and trust in the goodness of God, come what may! Perhaps we both shall profit." He shook his head. "I don't know why I just said such a thing."

"I have no problem with that," said the copper-merchant. "The only problem is that oil must be sold immediately. If not, storing it is a hard to do. Copper, however, has always been favored by God. Iron, copper, coal, silver, gold—everything that has blessedness is from the earth."

The oil-merchant laughed. "You know well how to bargain, but what we are talking about has no such need. We'll buy something and sell something. That which is desired greatly is always something that has to do with people's bodies, their food, and their dress! Isn't that right? It is possible there may not be a single thing made of copper in a house, but there is always oil. That's why oil will always have customers. Oil is like ready money. People use it all the time. Everyone has a need for it, but it cannot be mined like copper and used the next day. It is produced by the men's labor and is the product of the milk of cattle and sheep."

The copper-merchant laughed aloud. "Very well. If your heart is set on this deal, I agree. I suddenly had an impulse to accept your offer."

The oil-merchant trembled with delight and said: "God willing (*inshallah*), may God bless you and give your prosperity from this transaction! They say in the bazabbbar of Tabriz in Azeri Turkish Allah *barakat versin*! (God bless you!)—how good it is to know many languages!"

"Yes, learning languages is good," said the copper-merchant. "But I hardly know my own language very well! Anyway, let's make the formal contract to exchange our goods, and may you benefit from it also. That's my way all the time. I make a trade quickly and I never have any idea what I'm doing."

"All right," said the oil-merchant. "Let's make an account of the goods."

So they sat and took out pen and paper and their purchase documents and wrote out the transaction. As it happened, the goods were of equal value. The copper-merchant didn't really understand why they were making the exchange, but the oil-merchant knew that the sale of the oil would bring a loss and the copper would bring a profit.

However, something else happened after these events

while the ship was still a few leagues from its destination. During one dark night a storm arose and battered the ship. The hull sprang a leak and water began to enter the ship.

The captain struggled to keep the ship afloat. He assembled the passengers and crew and said to them: "Friends, all of our lives are in danger. If the ship is too heavy, it will sink. the only thing we can do is toss the cargo overboard to lighten the ship and save ourselves."

The two merchants and several of the others were distressed by this proposal.

"What's the difference," they asked, "if you throw our goods into the sea or we are drowned? If we lose our investments we'll be ruined and unable to live!"

"I understand," said the captain, "the loss of your capital is a very hard thing to endure. But, such words are for the city and in your home. Here we are in the sea and the most valuable thing we have is our lives. I don't care about the ship itself, but we may save ourselves if we lighten it. The hull is leaking badly. If the ship fills up with water, it will sink with us and all our goods. On board a ship the captain must make the decisions. If you try to prevent me, I'll order the crew to throw you into the sea!"

The two merchants shut up while the crew quickly threw all of the commercial cargo over the side; goatskins filled with butter and ghee, bales of copper utensils, and the goods and belongings of the others all went into the water. The ship was lightened and the damaged hull rose above the water line, so the captain was able to bring the ship close to the shore. The following day it anchored at their destination.

The oil and copper merchants were depressed, exhausted, and worried. They set foot on the shore, but all of their hopes had been dashed.

It was obvious that the copper which the oil-merchant had bought was now at the bottom of the sea, but the skins of animal oil that the copper-merchant had bought were floating on the surface. Little by little the wind and waves brought them towards the shore.

Whatever the sea takes from man, if unable to swallow, it casts on the shore. And oil floats on water!

So some of the goatskins filled with oil were cast upon the sand. The rest were picked up by boats from the sea's surface. And so the oil-merchant who, with all of his craft and shrewdness, had bought the copper of the copper-merchant lost everything. The copper-merchant, with all of his simplicity and honesty, was able to deliver his oil to the market and sell it at cost.

The plans that the clever oil-merchant made to outsmart his fellow were based upon the news that oil was selling at a low price in that place while copper was dear. But, the storm at sea had completely reversed the situation.

The simple copper-merchant said: "This disaster, while it didn't give me a profit, at least enabled me to keep my capital. I'm very sorry for what happened to you, but was it my fault? I didn't know what was going to happen, and you yourself had proposed that we exchange our goods."

The clever merchant said: "No, brother, no one is at fault. I had made all of my calculations and knew what I was doing, but I hadn't considered one thing, that the ship would be holed. Nor was it the captain's fault that the ship was too heavy to stay afloat. If he had not done what he did, we would not be here talking together. A lot of things happen like this in life. People call it bad luck, or good luck. I don't believe in luck, but these events have benefited you. In life we make plans, but there are always unplanned circumstances, such as earthquakes and storms, or drowning, or winning a lottery. I have no complaints, and I thank God that we survived. If a person is alive, he can rebuild his life!"

12
THE GIFT

Long ago there was an Arab who had spent his entire
life living with his family in the desert sands and
who had never seen a city. They lived in a tent near
a small stream that flowed from a spring at the base of a
hill and disappeared further down into the sand. They ate
mostly desert greens, locusts, and such things.

There was an ancient tree by the spring. It bore no
fruit. From a distance it looked green, but close up it was
dried up. The spring water was brackish and during the
heat of summer was so scanty that it could used only to
quench thirst and nothing else.

As long as the Arab could remember, this had been his
land and he didn't know that any other kind of country
was to be found in the wide world. So long as they haven't
seen anything better, people get used to their life as it is
and don't have higher hopes. The man was afraid to leave
his barren campsite because in his absence some greedy
person might come and occupy it.

When life became very hard, he would go to where he
could see the caravans crossing the desert. He would sit
there a long time watching them, thinking that perhaps

he might get some alms from the people in the caravan and hear some news of the outer world.

But the caravans passed infrequently. And so it was until one dry year the spring nearly dried up. It was reduced to a trickle. No matter how much they dug into the salty earth, they couldn't find any more water.

So the man threw a dry waterskin on his shoulders and set out to unknown parts in search of water. He walked for a long time until he was out of the sands of the desert and on a road. He met a man coming from the opposite direction and asked him: "Where does this road go? Is there any water or a campsite in that direction?"

He was looking for some place where there were plants and water.

The other traveler said: "A few leagues down, the road passes by a lake and eventually it reaches Baghdad."

This news pleased the Arab and he walked on until came upon a depression in which some rainwater had collected. Surrounding the depression there were some trees and grass. Since he had never seen a lake, the Arab thought that the small pool was a lake! He sat by it and splashed some of the water on his face. Then he drank the water and found it sweeter than any water he had ever tasted.

"What wonderful water!" he said. "Surely such water has come from heaven. When they talk about the water of heaven, and the Fountain of Kawthar, they speak the truth! How can there be such water in the world and we not know about it?"

He sat back and thought about his own miserable condition. If he were to fill his waterskin and return to his old campsite, what then? What would that accomplish? An accomplishment would be to make this water his capital for his own success.

So he said to himself: "It isn't right for me to take this water while the caliph of Islam hasn't heard about it! There is no one in this world more important than the caliph. He has a lot of power and wealth. It would be a good idea for me to fill my goatskin with this heavenly water and go to find the caliph and give it to him. After all, he may be the caliph, but he is also a human being, and he'll be delighted with the present and then. . . ."

There was no time for delay! He first wet the dry goatskin in the water then filled it. Then he slung it on his shoulders and headed for the Baghdad. On his way he asked everyone he met where the house of the caliph was until he finally approached the city.

As it happened, the caliph had left Baghdad to hunt. A tent had been pitched for him in the desert. The last time that the Arab had asked about the whereabouts of the caliph, someone pointed to the tent, saying: "Over there! That tent in the desert that you can see is the tent of the caliph. He himself is there. If you have some business with the caliph, there is no better opportunity for you to approach him than this!"

So the Arab thanked God for the lucky circumstance and made directly for the caliph's tent. But soldiers stopped him and asked him where he was going.

"I have an important news for the caliph!" the simple Arab replied. "It's good news for him!"

They escorted him to the presence of the caliph of Islam, the most powerful man in the world!

"You have some business with me?" the caliph asked the Arab.

"I have brought the caliph of Islam a gift from heaven," the Arab declared.

"From heaven?" asked the caliph.

"Yes," said the Arab happily. "From a place like heaven. Perhaps it was heaven itself."

The caliph thought that perhaps the Arab was mad. "Very well," he said. "Where is this gift?"

"Right here!" said the Arab straightening his shoulders. "This skin of water. No one in this world has tasted water better than this. Please, taste it. You see, when I reached heaven I thought it's a pity that I drink this water by myself and not think of the caliph."

The caliph realized that the Arab was a simple person who had spent his life in the dry desert and had never tasted sweet water and that he had brought the water in sincerity and to serve. The caliph ordered that a cup be brought. He poured some of the water into it and tasted it. It was rainwater and had the smell of mud and rotten grass.

"Delicious!" said the caliph. "We haven't heard of the desert heaven before this. You have done well in bringing us this gift. Now, tell me, is there anything you want in return for the trouble that you took to bring it here? What would you desire?"

"I desire only the good health of the caliph, but it has been a dry year and our spring has dried up. I was looking for water when I discovered this heaven. I didn't have a camel so that I could bring you a greater quantity of this wonderful water. But my family is waiting for me. I ask permission to leave and return to them."

The caliph poured what remained in his cup back into the goatskin and replaced the stopper. He turned to his courtiers and said: "Keep this water in a safe place."

Then he commanded them to make ready a camel with two filled waterskins, a purse of money, some bread and dates. Then he addressed the Arab in a friendly manner.

"These are the reward for the service you have performed for the caliph," he said. "But there is this condition: You must mount the camel and return the way you came and never enter the city again. Show no one else the location of the desert heaven, but use its water for yourself and your family."

The simple Arab accepted the gifts and prayed for the health, prosperity, and long life of the caliph. Then he returned happily to the place from which he had come.

After the Arab had gone, one of his courtiers said to the caliph: "It's obvious that that poor man had never seen any water better than this, but I don't understand why your majesty has ordered him not to enter Baghdad. Perhaps it would open his eyes and he would see a better life."

"It's better the way I arranged it," said the caliph. "That man wanted to perform a service and a good deed by bringing the skin filled with water to us. If he had continued on and had come to the broad, sweet waters of the Tigris River, he would have been embarrassed. I did not want to spoil his happiness. In return for his good deed, I tried to do a good deed for him that was the equal of his. Accepting gifts has rules. Let him be pleased with himself for a time with the service he has done us."

13
THE CHILD SCHOLAR

A long time ago in India there was a boy whose name was Raman. He was very smart and intelligent, and was always trying to learn some new thing.

When he was very small, he wanted to understand and know everything, to the point that he would continually pester his parents with questions. They didn't know what to do, because they didn't know the answers to many of his questions. Raman continually rained questions on his sister, his uncles and aunts, and the rest of his relatives.

Even though his father was an educated man and had read many books, he often found himself helpless to answer his son's unusual questions, yet his son still wanted to learn more every day.

"I don't know what will become of my boy," Raman's exasperated father would sigh. "Other children go out and play, but this one sits in front of us and asks questions such: 'Why doesn't an apple tree bear apricots?' 'Why does a mouse live in a hole and a sparrow in a tree?' 'Why does water dry up when it is spilled on the ground?' 'Why is the sun always round while the moon changes its shape?' 'Why does a stone sink in water while wood floats?' 'Why do people eat chickens and sheep and not cats?' God save us from this child who wants to poke his nose into everything!"

And that was how Raman was before he had learned to read and write!

Whenever someone gave him a toy, he would take it apart to see how it worked. Often he wasn't able to put them back together again. Other times he would make his own playthings out of bits of wood and paper and such like, which were really quite remarkable.

He had spent so much time with his mother that he had learned everything about running the household. He knew how to cook rice pilaf, how to make a black cherry sherbet, how to prepare vinegar from grapes. He learned how to remove pomegranate stains from white cloth. He knew how to made starch paste. . . .

He had learned so many things that whenever his aunts and uncles, or other relatives, visited his house, they enjoyed talking with him more than anyone else.

"Now," one of them once said to him, "what do you have to do to make one bean into twenty beans?"

"That's easy!" Raman exclaimed. "I'd plant the bean in the garden. It'll grow into a plant and produce more beans! I myself have planted beans, lentils, wheat, and even an apricot pit in a glass cup. I don't know why the apricot pit didn't grow, but all of the others did. I can give you some seedlings if you want."

Then Raman dashed off and came back with a glass. He had lined the glass with cloth, then poured some earth into it. He had put some seeds into the earth and then added some water. Now the green shoots of the plants were visible in the glass.

They all smiled and said: "God willing (mashallah)!

Our Raman is a great scholar! He examines and learns how to do everything!"

One day an aunt asked him: "Well, Raman, don't you ever want to go into the street and play with the other children?"

"Of course," Raman replied. "I know how to play everything. When the other children are playing and they argue about the rules or something, they always come to me and ask me to decide which side is right and which is wrong. They always accept my decisions because they know I don't fool around."

Raman looked up and continued:

"But playing in the streets has no benefit. My play is to learn everything people older than I know. Isn't that a kind of play? If you enjoy doing something, it becomes a kind of game, doesn't it?

"Yesterday father was carrying bricks up to the roof to build a wall. He got tired and I helped him. One, two, three. One by one I carried them up and father built the wall. While I was doing that I could see the kids playing in the street, but when evening came, father and I had built a wall and they hadn't done anything!

"Another time, the lady next door scolded the children because they were making so much noise in the street, but no one ever scolds me. Father said something to me that was very good. Do you know what he said? He said: 'God bless you, child. You are better than the other boys.'"

"Your father spoke the truth," his aunt said. "Raman is better behaved than all of the other children around here."

Raman was very fond of poems, riddles, puzzles, and tests of knowledge. Whenever he heard some one talking about something complicated, he listened very carefully so that he could learn something new and then ask others about it.

He learned to read and write when he was only five years old and started reading books ravenously. Even while his knowledge of the alphabet was not firm, he tried to read everything. Turning the pages he would discover on every page a dozen words he did not understand. Other books were written in languages he did not know. When he first came across such books, he went to his father:

"Father, why are these books written so strangely? Why don't the words have any meaning?"

His father explained:

"Son, our language is Hindi and it has it's own alphabet, which you know. But the world is vast and there are many other languages that are different from ours. Arabic, Persian, Turkish, Chinese, Greek, and many others. Some use our alphabet but we can't understand the words. We have to study the language if we want to understand the words. For example, we call water *pani*. The Persians call it *ab*, the Arabs *ma*, and the Turks *su*. After we learn such things, we can read their books."

"But some of them look so strange!" Raman protested.

"That's because they use different alphabets." smiled his father. "Some are written from left to right, others from right to left. Some are even written from top to bottom! Most European and Indian languages are written from left to right, but our alphabets are completely different. You have to learn the alphabets and the words to read many of the books you see."

When Raman understood that the people of the world spoke and wrote many different languages, he was still not satisfied.

"Father," he said, "why are there so many different languages? Wouldn't it be easier if everything spoke and wrote the same language?"

His father had grown tired of Raman's constant questions. In order to cut the discussion short, he said: "Of course, dear lad, it would be easier if everyone spoke and wrote the same language, but unfortunately that is not the way things are. When you get older you can learn as many languages as you wish. Many of these big books were not written for children. You should first read the books written for children, and then as you grow older, tackle the other books."

His father selected a number of books suitable for Raman's age and ability. They were mostly storybooks. "Now you read these books," Raman's father said, "and then tell me their stories and what they're about."

All of these books had been written by hand and contained colorful pictures.

But Raman finished reading those books quickly and then asked his father for more. Each book he read gave him new questions to ask his father: "Father, who was Plato?" "Father, what is a fire temple?" "Father, where is the city of Balkh located?" "Father, it says here that Solomon ruled over the *jinn* and mankind; what does that mean?"

Things were going along in that manner until he came across stories about the king of the fairies in a book. These amazed Raman more than anything he had read up until that time. There was a description of the happy, carefree lives of the *jinn* and fairies. They could do anything they wanted, and the king's daughter was more beautiful than any human girl. She could go from the east to west and travel about the land and sky in the blinking of an eye! She had a palace that was hidden from the eyes of all strangers. Anyone who knew her could summon her immediately if he possessed a single strand of her hair and burned it in fire. She would then fulfill all of the wishes of that person, who would become her friend. There were other stories about her like that.

The boy thought about the many strange and wonderful things in the world. So, where is this fairy princess who lives such a happy life and fulfills the wishes of people? Raman was eager to meet her and become her friend any way he could!

When night fell that day, Raman went to his father.

"Father, is the story about the king of the fairies true?"

"Well, they're stories," his father answered. "Fairy tales. Some of them are imaginary, some are true. If there is smoke, there may be fire!"

"Do you know the fairy princess, the daughter of the king of the fairies, father?"

"No," his father answered, shaking his head. "I don't know her. Fairies don't show themselves to just anyone. It's very hard to see them."

"But," Raman insisted, "what do the people do who see them? How do they get to know them?"

"They say that such people have to undergo many trials and difficulties," said Raman's father." They cannot eat meat. They must purify their souls. They must have a lot of knowledge about secret things. Not many know how to go about such things."

"But, father, can't you see the fairy princess if you want to? Can't I?"

"No, dear boy. Not just anyone can do that. It's very

hard. In our country there is only one person who knows about such a thing. Anyway, that's what people say, but the man himself never talks about it. He calls himself a philosopher, a doctor, and an astrologer, but from what he does people say that he knows the *jinn* and fairies. I said that these things have secrets. Anyone who knows the secrets doesn't tell anyone else. People who have learned the secrets of God have sealed lips and closed mouths."

Raman's young face became firm. "Well, I intend to do whatever it takes to learn those secrets. I must meet the fairy princess. So, who is that person you mentioned, father, who knows the *jinn* and fairies? Where can I find him?"

Raman's father realized that he was making problems for himself. With a tired sigh, he said: "My dear young man, do you know what? All of this is nonsense. There are no fairies. The king of the fairies is a lie. The princess is a lie. These are just made-up stories!"

Wide-eyed Raman listened to his father in astonishment. "Someone sits in a room and writes such things," his father continued, "using his imagination because he can do nothing better. They put the stories in a book and children read them for fun and so that they learn to read. That's all they are! The stories are ridiculous. I'm not going to let you read such foolish stories anymore. From now on you'll read only serious books. You'll learn some art or craft. All these stories about fairies and the like are not true." He shook his head in despair. "What a mess I've made for myself!"

Raman was disappointed with his father's words, but he hid his feelings in silence. However, he told himself: "It's not a lie! It would not be in a book if it weren't true!

For some reason, my father doesn't want to tell me how to meet the fairy princess or the man who knows her. By hook or by crook, I'm going to find her and get to know her!"

From that moment on, Raman thought only about *jinn* and fairies. He had to find a way to meet that wise man and learn the secrets of meeting them. He thought about it so much that he began to see the fairy princess in his dreams. She was like an angel flying about in the air, but whenever he tried to speak to her and catch hold of her clothes, she would fly away like a bird and disappear into the sky.

But the child who asked about everything and listened to the answers and understood them and learned from them had reached a dead end in his efforts to find out about the fairies. Everybody told stories about them, but no one knew even a single fairy personally. His father didn't want to talk about them anymore. After a few questions, it was clear to Raman that his mother didn't know anything about them. Nor did his aunt. His uncle said that only the good and wise knew about them.

"The wise know about these things," his uncle added, "but never give their secrets away."

"So I must rely upon tricks and cleverness to get them to reveal their secrets to me," Raman said to himself, his jaw set in determination. But it would not be an easy for him to meet the good and the wise.

Very well!

"I'll be extremely careful not to mention jinn and fairies any more," he said to himself. "I'll conceal my purpose and try to get to know some good and wise people."

So Raman said nothing more about them for a time

until gradually all that talk was forgotten. When he found a story about the jinn and fairies in a book, he gave it back to his father, saying: "I don't want to read this book! It's all nonsense, foolish fantasy! Such stories confuse a person's thinking. I must read useful things. What good are stories about *jinn* and fairies?"

These words pleased Raman's father. He continued to bring a variety of large, serious books. Raman would read them and then discuss them with his father. Gradually, Raman began to learn the mysteries of history, geography, medicine, and geometry. He became somewhat proficient in Greek and Sanskrit.

But with all of this, he still dreamed about learning the secrets of meeting a fairy princess. And he never forgot the words "the good and the wise."

One day Raman asked his father: "In this our time, who is the wisest of all men?"

His father shook his head. "Who knows? We don't know of all the wise men in the world. However, in our own country, people say that Jumna is the wisest man. they say he know everything there is to know today."

Raman tried to hide his excitement.

"Father," he asked, "is it possible that this Jumna who is the wisest is not also the best?"

His father nodded his head. "Yes, it is possible that that is also true."

"How odd!" exclaimed Raman. "When somebody knows more than others, he should also know good and evil better than others! How can he not be better than everyone else?"

"Look, my dear son," his father explained. "Knowledge is not the same as doing. Suppose that you are better at making mousetraps than anyone else. Is that a guarantee that you won't make a shoddy mousetrap and sell it cheaply?"

"Certainly that is possible," said Raman thoughtfully. "You mean that if I didn't use all the skill I possessed, my work wouldn't be good."

"Yes. So you see you can be the most skilled at what you do, but not the best. Knowledge is about study and learning, but goodness is about character and integrity. In the same way it is possible for some one to be better than others, but not so learned. Suppose you try your best to make a good mousetrap, but do not have the experience and skill. You're a good person, but not so learned and skillful."

"That's right," agreed Raman. "One other thing, father. In our age who do you think is the best person?"

"I don't know. We aren't familiar enough with all the good people of our age to be able to say which one is the best. But in our country, people say that that very Jumna is the also the best man. Of course knowledge can be quickly tested, but goodness cannot be determined so easily. Anyway, people say that Jumna is both the wisest and best man of our age in this land."

"Eureka! I've found him!" Raman cried in his heart. "Jumna is the person who can teach me the secrets of meeting the fairies."

Then he asked his father: "Where does this Jumna live?"

*****

"Why it happens that Jumna lives in our own city!"

said Raman's father. "He has his own house in the quarter by the river."

This information elated Raman. "Father," he asked, "do you like this Jumna, too?"

"Is it possible for some one not to like him?" asked his father by way of answer. "He is the source of great honor for our city. People go to him for advice and help when they have difficulties. He is a physician, an astrologer, a pharmacist, a wise man, and a philosopher. He is a believer and a dervish. He knows all mysteries, and he knows things that no one else knows. He can do things that no one else can do. They say he knows all languages. They say he converses with higher beings. They say many things about him."

Raman was almost jumping and crying out with joy, but he managed to control himself. He took a deep breath and asked:

"Tell me, father, if Jumna were your own son or brother, would you be happy?"

"What as question!" exclaimed Raman's father. "If he were just the nephew of the uncle of the uncle of our neighbor, it would make us all happy!"

Raman became quiet and fell into thought. He scribbled a few meaningless words on a piece of paper with the pen he had been holding in his hand as he pondered the matter. Suddenly he straightened up and said:

"Father, since things are thus, let's do something so that we can have a part of that happiness. Take me to Jumna so that I may study under him and learn all that he knows. Then I'll be a source of honor for you and our family. If I can't become this Jumna, I can at least become his student!"

His father laughed.

"I'm very happy that you have such a love for knowledge and wisdom, but this Jumna does not accept students. If he did, many important and powerful people would be glad to become his students. He is too busy to bother with students. Great doctors come to him for guidance in medicine. Scholars seek his advice in difficult questions. He doesn't have time to teach a child such as you. If that were not the case, I would be delighted for you to become his pupil."

"Very well," said Raman. "He doesn't have to teach me. If a person really wants to learn, he can observe carefully and learn much that way. Jumna certainly has things to do that require someone's help. I'm ready to work as his household servant, and I promise that I'll learn all of his knowledge after a time, even the secrets of the unknown!"

"That would be very difficult, son," said his father with a frown. "The problem is that Jumna prefers to live alone and doesn't want anyone to learn the secrets of his work. That's why he lives by himself. Even though he's very old, he does all of his own housework. He doesn't allow anyone to interfere in his life, so that no unworthy person can learn his secrets."

"That doesn't change things, father," Raman insisted. "It's wrong of him to keep other people from sharing his knowledge. A good man would want people to get more benefit from his wisdom."

"I don't know," replied his father with a shrug. "Perhaps he doesn't think it's proper. Perhaps he can't find any worthy person. There is some knowledge that it is better to keep from worthless persons; perhaps he is afraid that such people may learn his secret knowledge. I don't know, son, but I do know that the existence of such a man among us is very beneficial for the people."

"His usefulness is in his knowledge," said Raman. "You said that he is very old. God forbid, but if he should die, then he will take all of his wisdom to the grave. A person who does not teach his knowledge to others certainly will not write it in a book! That being the case, if anyone can learn his knowledge by any means possible, he will be doing mankind a service! Since this for the benefit of mankind, God will be pleased. So if I go and learn his wisdom and then teach others, in the future there will be many Jumnas, and that would be good!"

"That's so," said his father stroking his mustache, "how will you do it?"

"If you agree, it can be done," replied the boy confidently. "You say that he is a good man, but stingy with his wisdom. Doubtless he is a good man and wants the best for others. You can go to him and say that you have a son who is both deaf and dumb, and that no one will accept him as a pupil. Tell him that you are poor can't feed your son. Beg him to take your son into his house for the pleasure of God as a servant to wash and clean and just feed him. Plead with him so that his heart softens and he agrees. Use these words:

"Say: 'I have a deaf and dumb child;
I am poor and penniless, in a wretched condition.
No will take him on as an apprentice
If he doesn't get bread, he will perish
For God's sake, O wise man!
Take away this burden from me,
So that he may abide

A while in your service.
He'll sweep your house clean
And break up bread for the chickens.
When you arise from sleep he'll ready your shoes.
While you sit, he'll scrub your utensils.
When you go out, he'll shut the door.
He'll be busy with a hundred tasks for you.
He faces work as bravely as (the ancient hero) Rustam,
But he is watchful and humble.
He will not interfere with you:
His presence will be unnoticeable.
He is smart and intelligent, but deaf and dumb.
Do not disappoint my hopes;
It will make your life easier and also mine;
God will help both you and me!'"

Raman's father was thoughtful. "Son, even if this trick is not a sin, if he finds out, we shall be disgraced."

"Don't worry, father," said Raman. "I shall play my role so well that even Jumna's grandfather will believe that I am deaf and dumb. You know me and how good I am at such things. I don't have Jumna's knowledge, but I am more clever than he. I know how to convince him that I am indeed deaf and dumb. In that way I'll attain my goal and become a wise person."

"All right," said his father. "I'll do it. I only hope that I don't live to regret it."

Raman was overcome with joy and jumped into his father's arms. He kissed his face again and again and said: "What a good father you are! I am also a good child, the pupil of Jumna, the great Raman!"

*****

So, the father went to see Jumna and talk with him about his son. Raman was confident that everything would work out the way he had planned.

"If there is anyone who has any information about the fairy princess, it is that very Jumna!" thought. "I'm going to get what I want very soon. Tomorrow she will carry me on her wings to the ends of the earth and I'll be able to do anything I want!"

Two hours later Raman's father returned home with his news:

"Jumna has agreed. He said that children were talkative and curious and that he didn't need a helper to bother him and interfere with his work. But since you are handicapped, he could take you on for the pleasure of God. I told him a lot about you, how intelligent, smart, and polite you are. I told him that unfortunately you are deaf and dumb. No matter how much I tried I couldn't teach you to read and write. I told him that I had to use signs to make you understand things."

"Yes," cried Raman gleefully, "Raman is deaf and dumb! He was born deaf and dumb, not hearing the cattle and as silent as a turtle. Of course he wouldn't know how to read and write! Yes, that is Raman! The great Raman is mute and illiterate! I shall endure of all of this because I must become a learned man. O God! How happy I'll be.

"But, father, be careful. If you visit me there, don't talk with me. Always remember that your Raman is deaf and dumb. Don't spoil my plans, or Jumna will take me by the ear and throw me out of his house!"

"No, no!" protest his father. "I'll keep my wits about me.

Yallah! Let's go!"

"Wait a moment, I have to collect my books."

"Books? What books?" cried his father. "You're supposed to be illiterate!"

"The books that I'll take with me will prove that I can't read," said Raman triumphantly. "I'll take pieces of this old, torn notebook and draw meaningless crooked lines in it. If Jumna asks you about it, explain to him that when Raman watches me writing in my notebooks, he tries to imitate me. He likes to do that, but he doesn't know how to write. Then you'll show Jumna the notebook and he'll see my scribblings and believe that I don't know the difference between a ball and a bull. Then he won't hide his secret writings from me!"

"Naughty boy!" his father laughed. "You know well how to play a role!"

Raman continued to scribble and draw lines in his notebook, then he announced: "I'm ready to go, father." He paused a moment. "By the way, father, did you tell Jumna my name?"

His father considered a moment, then shook his head. "No, not yet."

"Then you mustn't tell him my real name," Raman said, his eyes gleaming. "Tell him that my name is Himalaya, or something like that."

"Why a false name?"

"Because, father, he may call out to me at some time. If he says 'Himalaya,' I won't be caught off guard. But if says 'Raman,' I might answer suddenly without thinking, because I am used to answering to that name. I won't make such a mistake if he calls me Himalaya."

Raman's father was amazed at his son's foresight.

"You're right, Raman," he said. "If he asks me your name, I'll give him a different name. But what will he have to do with your name? If he thinks you are deaf, knowing your name is useless."

*****

So Raman and his father left home and headed for Jumna's house. On the way, Raman started to practice his role as a deaf and dumb person and began to talk with his father with movements and gestures instead of words. Then the reached Jumna's house.

Upon entering, Raman placed his two hands on his chest as a sign of respect and bowed. Then he stood quietly before Jumna. Raman's father greeted Jumna and showed his respect. Then he spoke about his son to the old man:

"This is my unfortunate son, deaf and dumb. I place him in your care. I hope that you will be pleased with him. He's a good lad, but what can I do with him? The poor boy came into the world without the use of his tongue. Even though he can't speak, I've tried to teach him to write, but he can't learn anything. Perhaps, it is my fault that I do not know how to teach him. Anyway, instead of learning the alphabet, he draws senseless lines in his notebook. Take a look. . . ."

The father took the notebook from his son's hand and showed it to Jumna.

"He's very fond of this notebook, sir," Raman's father added. "He likes to scribble in it. It's a pity that he can't learn to read and write. It is useless, sir. I've tried everything."

Jumna looked at Raman thoughtfully, then said. "I see."

Then he took a box of hard candy from a shelf and held it out to Raman and his father. Raman took one piece and then, bowed to kiss Jumna's hand respectfully. But Jumna pulled his hand away first and said to Raman's father:

"Let me give this lad something to do to keep him busy."

He picked up a sickle from the far end of the room and took Raman by the arm. Then he led the boy outside into the garden and then he showed Raman how to cut the tall grass with the sickle. Using gestures, Jumna ordered the boy to cut the grass wherever it had grown too tall. Jumna watched him work for a bit, then returned to the room where he had left the father.

"In my opinion, the lad is very intelligent," Jumna told Raman's father. "You have been talking about his reading and writing, which is something different. Don't worry, a deaf and dumb child can be taught to read and write, but he needs a proper teacher. It isn't something that you can do. If he is a good student, and I am satisfied with him, I'll gradually teach him myself.

"You must only instruct him that this is no place for playing around. I have not the patience to take care of an infant. There is an old village woman who cooks and sews for me. They can work together and help each other. I'll also ask her to watch over him. He probably knows what how to look after himself, doesn't he?"

"Yes, sir," replied Raman's father, "he knows how to look after himself! As far as I could make him understand, I have told him how to behave in your house. Rest assured that he is a quiet, reasonable, hardworking child. I hope that he has the ability to learn under your instruction and to be grateful for trouble as long as he lives. Now, with your permission, I shall leave him in your hands and take my leave."

Jumna touched his beard and looked at the father.

"By the way, you haven't told me his name."

"His name? His name?" the father stammered. "His name, sir, is Himalaya. But he himself doesn't know what it is. What can the poor lad know of his name. . .?"

"You are right," said Jumna. "That's all for now. You can visit your son whenever you wish, but it his mother or others want to visit him, it would be better if you take him to them. I don't like a lot of visitors in this house."

"As you wish," said Raman's father with a slight bow. He said his farewells and left.

*****

Raman was still cutting grass in the garden. "From this moment on I must remember that I cannot hear or speak," he reminded himself. He might be tested at any time. "I mustn't pay any attention to any sound whatsoever. If I am called, I must not answer, even if he should hit me."

As it happened, Jumna was thinking about the same thing. He wanted to find out if the boy was completely deaf. By way of a test, he opened a window and looked into the garden where he saw Raman cutting the grass. The boy was not looking in his direction.

Jumna called him: "Himalaya! . . . Himalaya!"

Raman knew that he was being called and he knew that he must pretend to be deaf.

Jumna took a clay jar and threw it at a spot behind Raman. the jar shattered with a loud noise, but Raman paid no attention.

"Himalaya!" Jumna called. "What was that noise? Was something broken?"

Raman continued working and did not reply.

Jumna smiled to himself. "Poor boy," he thought. "Such an innocent child! What a pity!" Then he returned to his own work.

When Raman finished cutting the grass, he raked the ground and threw the rakings into a basket that had been place for that purpose at the edge of the courtyard. He picked up the broken pieces of the jar and placed them beside the basket; then he returned to the room where he had met Jumna. He returned the sickle to its place and getting the old man's attention pointed out the basket full of cuttings and the pile of broken pieces of clay. Using signs, he asked Jumna what he wanted him to do with them.

Jumna took out and showed him where to throw the trash. After that was done, Raman washed his hands and went back to the room and stood quietly at one side.

Jumna started to talk with him, asking questions: "Very good, dear lad. What is your name?"

Raman stared at Jumna, but said nothing. Jumna said: "If you're tired, you may sit on that stool."

Raman continued to stand as though he had not heard anything.

Jumna got up and motioned for the boy to follow him. He took Raman to a room the four walls of which were lined with books. It was Jumna's library! It was a large room with shelves and cabinets, all full of books. A lot of dust had collected on the books. Picking up a dust cloth, Jumna took out a few volumes off the shelf, dusted them and then replaced them. He indicated to Raman that he should dust all of the books. He himself took a volume and went to the window and began to leaf through its pages.

Raman set to work. He saw that on the spine of each book a label had been pasted a couple of inches from the top giving the name of the book. Some of the books had been replaced upside down. He took down all of the books from a section and then cleaned them on the floor. When he replaced them he put them all in upside down. He did this on purpose so that Jumna wouldn't learn that he could read.

When he had finished he went to Jumna and pulled at the old man's sleeve. He wanted to Jumna to inspect his work. Jumna examined the shelves and laughed. He pulled out one of the volumes and pointed to the label. He showed Raman which way the books should be returned to the shelves.

Raman nodded to indicate that he understood.

After watching Raman work for a few minutes, Jumna left the boy to finish by himself and went back to his own room to continue the work he had left there. Meanwhile, now alone in the library, the boy was busily reading the names of the books as he replaced them on the shelves.

"What marvelous books!" he said to himself. "What wonderful knowledge is contained in them. Everything!" But Raman noticed that the handwriting on the labels was not very good.

"Is it possible that such a wise man's handwriting could be so bad?" Raman asked himself. "Look at this one: The Life of the Prophets. And this one: The Tale of Socrates.

And here: Magical Medicines. But where is there anything about the secrets of the fairies?"

It was nearly noon when the old woman came into the house from the street. Jumna called her and told her about Raman. Then he said:

"The lad is working in the library today. He will be there from now on, but remember that he is deaf and dumb. Keep an eye on him. If you need him to help you in anything, just show him what you want him to do. His name is Himalaya, but that won't help you, because he doesn't even know it! Show him where the water and lavatory is, and where he is to sleep. Try to get him to talk if you can, but in any case take care of him. He seems to be a good boy."

"As you wish," said the old woman. She took a look into the library but did not go in. She was not supposed to enter that room.

Then she started her own housework. At noon she took the boy into the kitchen for his lunch. She tried to get him to speak, but was not successful. That afternoon she said to Jumna:

"Sir, that boy is very quick and smart. He does everything I tell very well, but the poor boy is like a doll, deaf and dumb. May God heal him!"

For the first few days Raman was very careful to show to his new master and the old woman that he indeed could not hear or speak. He reminded himself constantly that he might be tested at any time. And in this he was not wrong.

On the second day, while he was putting the books of the library in order and cleaning them, he dropped one of the handwritten books and the leaves of the volume fell apart and scattered on the floor. He looked at the book and saw that the pages were not numbered.

In the old days, when books were not printed but copied by hand instead, it was the custom to write the first word of the next page at the bottom of the preceding page in place of a number. In the same way, the last word of the previous page was written at the top of the next page. Raman knew that he could put the pages in the right order by matching the key words. He knew how to do this because he and read many old handwritten books like that one, but it would take a lot of time.

If someone should look into the library while he was doing this, that person would understand that Raman could read. At the same time, he could not leave the pages of the book scattered over the floor. Someone might already have glanced in through the door or window and seen the mess!

So Raman pretended to cry and went to Jumna's room. Making signs and pulling at the old man's sleeve, Raman led him to the library and showed him the pages of the book on the floor.

Now Jumna loved his books very much. When he saw what had happened, he grew angry and cuffed Raman on the neck.

"If you do anything like this again, I'll take you by the ear and throw you out of the house!" Jumna cried angrily.

Since Jumna had pointed to the door, Raman ran to the door, looked into the corridor, then came back. With his hands and the expression on his face he tried to say to Jumna: "I don't understand what you want. . . ."

Jumna sat and began to put the pages in order. Raman helped by collecting the pages into a pile, some of them backwards, others upside down, and then handing them to

Jumna. The master then arranged them and put them in their proper place. As he did so, he muttered: "Look at me, trying to do a good deed!"

It was plain that he was very upset, but when he looked at the tear-filled eyes of Raman, he regretted his anger. He touched the boy's arm and said: "It's all right. Don't be upset, but be more careful."

Remembering Raman's deafness, he sighed to himself, saying: "Of what use are my words?"

After finishing the task of sorting out the book, he returned to his own room to continue his studies.

*****

For the next few days, whenever Raman had no other chores to do, he was in the library cleaning and straightening the books. By now the old master and the old woman who kept his house in order for him were certain that Raman, whom they called Himalaya, was truly deaf and dumb. Raman had learned all of his duties and they no longer paid much attention to him.

But Raman was not idle for a moment. Though he did everything he was told very well, at the same time he was working to achieve his own goal. He washed pots and pans. He swept the house. He dusted books, the master's desk, and arranged his writing equipment. He carried water into the house. He helped the old woman wash and cut greens and vegetables in the kitchen. He accompanied Jumna on his walks. He learned when he should carry the books from his master's work room back to the library. He knew when to lock up the library and when to eat his meals. He knew when he should go to sleep and when he should wake up in the morning.

The only thing he did not do was talk. Whenever someone knocked at the door or spoke to him, he pretended to be deaf. He did respond to the commands of his master or the old woman until they used signs to explain to him what they wanted him to do. They were thoroughly convinced that he was deaf and dumb.

Everything was going according to Raman's plan.

*****

When Raman first arrived at Jumna's, whenever a visitor came to see the master, Raman was sent out of the room. But after a while, Jumna no longer bothered to do this and conversation would continue even when he was present. For his part, Raman would sit in a corner of Jumna's room like a statue if he had nothing else to do. He heard and understood everything that passed between Jumna and his visitors.

In this way, Raman learned many secrets about life and knowledge without giving himself away.

People came to Jumna for medicine. They brought him problems which Jumna solved with them. They came to him for advice. They asked him various questions. Raman thought that Jumna was an incredible man to possess so much wisdom. In Raman's view, above all else, Jumna was a physician, and the most important thing that he was learning was how to prepare remedies and treat sickness.

Now Raman was always present in Jumna's room like a servant. He saw the practical side of Jumna's knowledge in his treatment of the visitors, many of whom were really patients. And Raman began to study the theory of this knowledge by reading the big volumes he found in the library.

He liked it best when the master went out to visit the sick in their homes. Then Raman was left alone and he had a good chance to read in the library. He spent most of this valuable time, however, in searching for the secret of meeting the fairy princess. He had looked at every book on the shelves and found nothing about this extremely important matter.

Then his eye fell on some large chests piled in a corner of the big room. Whenever the master wanted something from them, he would first shut the door and then open them himself with a key. Before opening the library door again, he would lock them up.

"Whatever secrets there are, they are kept in those chests," Raman said to himself, studying the locked boxes.

*****

Once a month Raman's father would come and ask Jumna to let him take Raman home to see his mother. On the first occasion, as soon as they were in the street, his father asked how things were going, but Raman did not answer.

The father took Raman by the arm and said sternly: "I'm talking to you. Are you deaf?"

Then Raman laughed: "I'm sorry, father. Peace be upon you! Everything is going well, but I play so much at being deaf and dumb, that I've gotten used to it. A person who does something all the time gets used to it. Anyway, everything is fine and I'm learning a lot."

Whenever Raman visited his home, he talked about the

wonderful things he had seen and heard. He made compounds and magical medicines. He talked so grandly and with such authority that his family and relatives were astonished. Gradually he became the family doctor. Whenever one of them needed medicine, he came to Raman for it and for treatment. They were all happy that Raman had become so learned even though he was still a youth.

Time passed. Raman had read so many books of medicine and had learned so much from watching Jumna treat his patients, the little by little he began to really enjoy being a doctor. At first he had been searching for a fairy princess, but now his surroundings played an important part in his fate and were turning him into a physician.

The best day of all in this time of learning was when he got his hands on the keys to the trunks. It happened in this way:

Jumna had gone on a trip for several days and had instructed the old woman not to open the door of the house to anyone. While Jumna was away there was little work in the house. To feel safe and secure, she locked the front door from the inside and tied the key to the small bag she had hung around her neck like a necklace. She prepared light meals and ate them with Raman. The rest of the time she sat and napped.

Raman would sit and draw meaningless lines in his notebook, and then pretend to fall asleep until the old woman left him alone and went to her own room to sleep.

Then Raman got busy with his studies. While looking at some books that Jumna had set on his table, Raman suddenly found his hands on the keys to the trunks in the library!

"No more time for sleep," Raman told himself, handling the keys eagerly.

As soon as the old woman had gone to her room to sleep, Raman went into the library and hung a thick curtain over the window so that light of his candle would not be seen by anyone outside. Then he lit the candle he had brought from home and opened the chests and began to search for the secrets they contained.

There was no gold or jewels in those chests, but Raman found a treasure far more valuable to him: handwritten books, documents, and other papers the like of which he had never seen! They represented the real wealth and experience of the wise and learned master. Raman realized that Jumna was right to have put his most precious books in these chests. He began to read and learn the things that were the fruit of a lifetime of study!

The most interesting of all to Raman were Jumna's journals. In them he revealed many secrets about himself. Raman wondered why Jumna had written them. Perhaps he wanted to leave something of himself in the world after his death. But why hide them? Perhaps he hoped to have the time to organize them properly and write an autobiography.

As he read the journals, Raman began to understand just how good a man Jumna was. In them Jumna commented about people he had met, things that had happened, what people said, and ideas and beliefs. As he read, Raman found himself agreeing with Jumna's judgments.

So, while Jumna was absent on his trip, Raman spent the nights reading the books and papers in the chests and slept during the day. At night he was a student; during the day he rested. As soon as the first light of dawn appeared around the corners of the curtain he would hang over the window, he would close up the chest, hide his notes, and remove the curtains.

Then he would go to his own room where soon the old woman would come and shake his arm to awaken him. He would smile, yawn, and thank her with gestures. He counted himself fortunate that the old woman was lazy and slept as much as a rabbit. If she had been wakeful, he wouldn't have been able to read the master's books. Sometimes a lazy friend is a blessing, as a lazy teacher can be! A lazy teacher often leaves the work to the students who then have more time to practice their lessons.

*****

By the time Jumna returned from his trip, Raman had finishing reading all the books in one of the chests and had filled a notebook the size of a book with his notes! He had mastered the contents of those books and now he understood the source of Jumna's wisdom. As soon as Raman saw his master he ran to him and kissed his hand to show his happiness at the master's safe return. But Raman really wanted to thank him for going on the trip.

But there no more trips for some time and Raman had to wait a long while before he could read the books in the second chest.

But the time inevitably passed. Raman saw that he had learned all of the master's works that he had been able to lay his hands on. But there was still no hint about the secrets of the fairy princess! There had been nothing in the books he had read. Nothing in the papers and notes. And no one had ever brought up the subject in his hearing.

Raman decided he would have to resort to some trick or device to find out what Jumna knew about the fairy princess. "How can I get him to talk about it?" he asked himself as he pondered the problem.

Then he thought of a plan.

*****

The next time his father came to take him to see his mother, Raman spoke with his aunt, the sister of his mother:

"Dear aunt, they say that when a person has a problem there is no one that can be trusted more than an aunt. I, too, would like to ask you something, but you mustn't tell my father!"

His aunt smiled, pleased at being singled out for Raman's confidence.

"Ask away, my dear nephew," she said. "An aunt can keep your secrets better than anyone. There are things a child finds hard to say to his mother or father. Friends not from the family might mislead you. The best advice always comes from aunts!"

Raman was encouraged by these words.

"This is my problem, dear aunt," he said. "Jumna knows about fairies and solves many problems for them, but I can't ask him anything about them. I want you to help me so that I can learn their secrets. Now, I've noticed that Jumna is very fond of honey. I want to give him a jar of honey and ask him about the secrets of meeting the fairies."

"How can I ask him about that?" asked his surprised aunt.

Raman smiled confidently.

"I'll tell you how to ask him."

He explained his plan to his aunt and they agreed that she would go to Jumna two days later and say to the old man what Raman had taught her. Then they would see what the result would be.

*****

On the appointed day, Raman's aunt took a jar of the best honey and went to Jumna's house. When she saw the famous man, she said:

"O great teacher! I've had a strange dream and I've come to you to ask you what I should do. In the dream I saw a fairy princess, the daughter of the king of the fairies, flying in the sky. Now, I have suffered from night-blindness for many years. In my dream I thought that she had come to heal me, but as much as I called out to her, she did not reply. When I implored her, she said: 'If you wish me to cure you, you must bring a jar of the purest honey to Jumna and ask him the secret of how to meet me.' Then she disappeared from my sight and I woke up. Now, tell me, what should I do?"

At that time Raman was busy in a corner of the room straining a potion that Jumna had concocted. He was listening very carefully.

Jumna laughed.

"Woman!" he said, "the dream you saw was from your own imagination. Perhaps you ate too much the night before. Don't eat so much before you go to bed and you'll sleep better."

He chose a bottle of medicine from a shelf and handed

it to her.

"Take this medicine and put two drops into your eyes every night for a month. Your eyes will get better, God willing. And, sister, it is better that you not talk about the fairies. I thank you for the gift of honey."

"But, sir, what about my dream and the fairy princess? She herself told me to go to you. How did she direct me to you?"

"Your medicine is in that bottle," said Jumna. "I am a well-known doctor. You probably heard my name and thought to ask me for medicine for your eyes. Thinking of that, you saw the fairy princess in your dreams. That's all it was. I don't like to talk about such things as fairies."

Raman's aunt did not know what else to say. She thanked the doctor and left. For his part Raman realized that Jumna would not be so easily drawn out about the fairy princess.

Now Raman was too resolute to get discouraged by this failure. A clever lad has no need of *jinn* and fairies, but he really wanted to learn their secrets. However, he had to admit to himself that his first plan had not worked.

On another day something else happened. Early in the morning the governor of the city himself sent a message to Jumna, saying that his daughter was seriously ill. It also happened that on that day Jumna himself was not well, but he knew that he had to see the girl and try to help her.

Sometimes Jumna had Raman accompany him on his visits to the sick, but on that day he went by himself. Raman was upset at this. He wanted very much to know what the girl's sickness was and how Jumna would cure her.

A few minutes after Jumna left, the old woman also

went out. Raman knew she wouldn't return until it was nearly noon. He immediately ran to her room and dressed himself in a veil and woman's shoes. Then he ran to the governor's house in this disguise. He found many women there. Mixing with the women, he managed to enter the room of the sick girl and watch Jumna treat her. The governor's regular doctor was already there.

Raman recognized the illness as something he had already learned about. He had read about it in the books and seen Jumna treat it in his patients. The girl had the croup, a bad cough and a very sore throat. It is dangerous because it makes breathing very difficult and can block air to the lungs. It must be treated quickly. With a small operation, a tube is inserted into the throat to make breathing possible.

Now it happened that the girl had another, more obvious problem, an ugly sore on her throat that needed a poultice. This attracted the attention of the doctor who had first come to the girl's aid first, causing him to neglect the far more dangerous breathing problem.

And, Raman saw, Jumna was making the same mistake!

Sick himself, the old man was not thinking clearly. Neither the first doctor nor Jumna had seen the more serious problem. The two doctors cleaned and treated the sore and prepared to leave the patient. But she was choking and would soon choke to death if her throat wasn't opened.

Raman knew that Jumna's diagnosis was wrong. There was nothing else for him to do. He went in his girl's dress to Jumna and whispered to him: "Dear master, you have treated the swelling correctly, but the real problem of the girl is that she is choking to death! Have you looked inside her throat?"

Without looking at the speaker, Jumna quickly looked at the girl's throat.

"You're right! You're right! I almost forgot! I'm getting old and I'm not well. Whoever you are, you're an angel sent to save the girl's life! Bless you, intelligent girl, may God grant you happiness!"

The crisis prompted Jumna to work quickly. The wife of the governor happened to overhear Raman's words. Raman was so happy that his master had paid attention to him that his eyes filled with tears. He had nothing more to do and decided to leave the room and get back to the house before he was discovered. But the governor's wife went after the disguised boy and took his arm in the hallway.

"Whose daughter are you?" she asked Raman. "I must get to know you. It was you who saved my daughter's life!"

Still wearing the veil, Raman pulled it around him and said: "If my words have helped you, it is better that you not ask about me. Let me go. You must not know me. It will be bad. Jumna is a great doctor. Did you not see how he accepted the truth? Please, let me pass."

"We can't let you go," insisted the governor's wife. "All right, we won't tell Jumna who you are, but I must know who the savior of my daughter is! If you won't tell me who you are, I'll keep you here until I find out!"

"No, that would be worse," pleaded Raman desperately. "All right, I'll tell you. I'm Jumna's student. Everything I know I have learned from him. But he must not learn of this. I don't want to make him unhappy. You see, I work in his house, but he thinks that I am deaf and dumb. He often takes me with him, but today he didn't. I dressed as a woman I and came by myself. I'm not a girl, I'm a boy. I came to learn and I didn't know that it was God's will that I would come and say something useful. Now, please let me go. I have to be in his house. Jumna must not learn that it was I who spoke. I owe him a lot. Please don't give me away."

"I understand," said the governor's wife. "You may go, but we shall never forget you."

*****

Raman got back to the house before his master returned a little while later. Jumna was very upset with himself and refused to see anyone else that day. That night he went to the library and opened one of the chests. He took out his diary and wrote in it for a while. Then he replaced and locked the chest.

The next day Raman found an opportunity to open the chest and read what Jumna had written in his dairy. This is what he had written:

"Something strange happened today. I was not feeling well and I failed to diagnose the illness of the governor's daughter when I went to his house. But there was girl there among the women who pointed out my mistake to me. If she had not spoken, the governor's daughter would not have been saved.

"It was an odd thing. I have not made such a mistake until this day. I have not been able to find out who the girl was or where I could find her. No one knows anything about her. It is as though she were an angel who had come to save the life of the sick girl and afterwards vanished! What does it mean?

"A few days ago a woman came to me and asked about fairy princesses. I do not understand how she knew that I was fond of honey! Was she just imagining things, or was there more to it? I do not know. When I was young I suffered much to see the fairies, but nothing happened. Was that girl who came today the answer to all those prayers long ago when I was very young? Who else there could have understood the problem of the sick girl?

"I do not understand. I wish to God that whoever it was would come to me so that I could kiss her hand and praise her properly! It is a shame that I do not know her. If she was a fairy princess, why did she wait until now to come to me when I am an old man? Will she come again? I would give much to learn what is behind all of these mysterious events."

Raman was stunned as he read those pages.

"How strange! So a fairy princess is something that even Jumna knows nothing about! He thinks that I might be a fairy princess! If that is the case, maybe I should let him know who I really am. Should I, or shouldn't I? Will that upset him or please him? I don't know what to do."

Raman continued to think his dilemma.

"At least it's good that I've learned the truth about the fairy princess. She's just something imaginary. After all, it was I who got my aunt to visit Jumna with the honey, and it was I who saw what was wrong with the governor's daughter. Everything I knew about treating sickness I had learned from Jumna. So, for me, Jumna is the fairy princess as I was for him! "

But Raman was cautious and not in a hurry to tell the truth to Jumna until he had thought the matter over very, very carefully for a few days. But he noticed that Jumna continued to be upset and when Raman heard that the governor's daughter had fully recovered, he decided to tell his master the truth.

*****

The next day when the old woman came to wake Raman up, he said: "Good morning. How are you?"

The old woman gaped at him in astonishment and fright, but she managed to calm herself and said: "I'm very happy, Himalaya, but how is that you have suddenly found your tongue?"

"Last night the fairy princess came to me in a dream and made me well," Raman said.

The old woman ran to Jumna to give him the good news. Jumna, too, was astonished.

"What wonderful things are happening these days!" the old man exclaimed. "Bring Himalaya to me that I may see him."

Raman entered his master's room and greeted him and then said: "Dear master, I want to thank you for all of your kindnesses. You are a very good man."

The master was more than a bit surprised. He replied to Raman's greeting with affection, and said: "I am very happy to see that you can now speak, Himalaya. Tell me what has happened to you that you have found your tongue?"

"Dear master," said Raman, "I don't know whether my telling you the truth will make you happy or whether I should tell a lie."

"What is this you're saying, lad?" asked Jumna. "I don't want to hear lies. Of course the truth will make me happy."

Raman took a deep breath and began:

"Master, you have been very good to me in the time I have been living in your house. I shall not forget that as long as I live, and I shall always pray for you. But I know a secret which you do not know. I know who the fairy princess is that you have been thinking about. If I may be sure that you will not become upset, I am prepared to introduce her to you."

"Why should I be upset?" asked Jumna, his brow wrinkled as he tried to understand what Raman was driving at. "But how do you know the fairy princess? From dreams? I would really like to know."

"No," said Raman, shaking his head. "Not from dreams. By daylight. But I can only tell you under certain conditions. You must promise not to be angry with me. You must promise to forgive me and keep me as your student and not withdraw your love from me. Those are the conditions."

"I promise," said Jumna. "You have never done anything bad to me. If you have made any mistake, I forgive you. But only if you speak the truth."

"I promise to tell the truth," Raman said. "I got you to promise me so that I could tell you the truth. First, you should know that the girl who spoke with you in the room of the governor's daughter had learned about medicine from you."

Jumna stared at Raman in surprise. Then he asked: "How can that be?"

"Please," Raman said. "I'll explain. Let me bring her to you, then I'll tell you everything."

Raman ran to the old woman's room, put on the shoes and veil, and ran back to Jumna.

"Didn't she look like this?" Raman asked him.

"Yes," said Jumna. "Something like that."

"Not 'something,'" cried Raman. "Exactly! Dear master, that girl wore these very shoes and this very veil! They belong to the old woman who works in your own house! I was that girl! I went there dressed like this. It was I who spoke to you. Whatever I know about medicine I have learned from you. The governor's wife found out the truth, but I was afraid you would be angry at me."

"But, but," stuttered Jumna, "when did you start to speak and why didn't you tell me so that I could share your happiness?"

"You are like my father to me," Raman said. "I came here because I wanted to learn how to meet the fairy princess. I pretended to deaf and dumb so that I could learn the secret. That was because people said that if any-one knew the fairies it would be you and only you, but that you wouldn't tell anyone. I am very ashamed of the trick I played, but I didn't want to hurt anyone. I just wanted to learn the secret of meeting the fairy princess. Instead I learned some part of your wisdom. I went to the governor's house to learn more about medicine, but it was as though God had sent me there to save the sick girl and to do you credit. I am very happy that my studies with you benefit-ed the girl.

"My crime was that I pretended to be deaf and dumb. But why did I do that? People said that you wouldn't teach anyone your knowledge and I wanted to learn. I don't know whether I did right or wrong, but anyway today you have a pupil standing before you who is proud to be your student. My real name is Raman."

"I am proud to have such a student," said Jumna,

putting his hand on Raman's young shoulder, "a student who is ready to make such efforts in his search for knowledge. Forget about what people say. Perhaps I was afraid my knowledge would fall in the hands of the unworthy, but now I thank God Most High that it will be in the hands of such a person as you."

Then Jumna laughed. "So you knew how to read and write from the first day you came here!"

"Yes, sir," said Raman. "I've read a lot of books.

"The books in my chests?" asked Jumna with a twinkle in his eye.

"I read those in one of the chests," Raman said. "The chest that has your diary in it. But I haven't read those in the other chest. I was looking for the secrets of the fairy princess, but I don't need those any more."

"No one needs such things," said Jumna. "You know, even I was thinking about her recently, but the fairy princess is really knowledge and learning. They help a person do anything. Just as they will make you a learned man, the pride of your family and your teacher."

"I am ashamed that I cannot repay you for your goodness," Raman said.

"You will repay me by using your knowledge to make other people happy," said Jumna. "I consider myself fortunate that my learning and my books will help make a great scholar like Raman!"

*****

Well, we don't know whether the governor's wife remembered Raman and showed her gratitude to him or not. But we do know that Jumna and Raman considered themselves happy and fortunate as long as they lived.

After all, the person is happiest who has faith and wisdom, who uses his wisdom for the good of others.

14

THE LESSON OF THE MAN IN THE FELT CAP

A long time ago, there was a ruler of Nishabur who wanted to be serene and kind, but no matter how much he tried, he could not. It was his nature to be impatient and hot-tempered. Whenever he heard something he did not like, he would get angry and issue strict and harsh orders that he would later regret. If he was unable to get his way, he would burn with anger and behave as though it was the end of the world and nurse a grudge at his failure for the rest of his life.

By the same token, when he was happy and something pleased him, he would forget himself and his dignity and frivolously make sport with others. Afterwards he would be regret his behavior. He himself realized that his excess of harshness and indulgence was making others unhappy.

One he sat down and "made his hat the judge." That is, he thought seriously about his behavior and his situation.

"It's very bad for me to be so temperamental," he told himself. "Why can't I be even-tempered and think before I act? Perhaps my nerves are weak. Perhaps it is in my heart. It would be better if I went to the doctor. Maybe he has some medicine to calm me down."

So he invited the most famous physician of Nishabur to his palace and described his problem to him. Then the ruler asked: "What medicine should I take?"

"As far as I understand," said the doctor, "there is nothing wrong with you physically that I could treat with medicine. There is no doubt that you have a problem, but it is not something for which you can take medicine. It has to do with bringing up and character. When you were a child you were spoiled and always got your way. You did not mature as you should. In order to do so, you must read a lot of books containing the words of the wise and the lives of the great. You must find a motto to live by that will inspire you to patience and restraint. You must keep it before you always and learn not to lose yourself in sorrow and joy. For a sick soul, you need spiritual medicine."

"That's right," said the ruler. "I should have known that."

He summoned a preacher and a philosopher and told them about his problem.

Said the preacher: "There are many rules of character, your excellency. One of them, which might be good for your problem, is to visit graveyards and remember death. Do not forget the consequences of deeds, and know that neither sorrow nor joy lasts forever. Then perhaps you will find wisdom and peace."

"But I cannot go to a graveyard every time I feel sorrow or joy," protested the ruler. "I need something simpler that I can always keep with me."

"Said the philosopher: "In my opinion it would be better for you keep a circle of wise men about you and seek their advice before you take any action. Only issue orders with their agreement. These wise men will stop you from being too strict or too easy. They will console you in your sorrow and advise you when you show pride."

"But if I only give orders when the wise men approve, what kind of a governor would I be?" demanded the ruler.

"I know the difference between good and bad," he continued, "but when I get very angry or happy, I forget myself. I want something that I can have inscribed upon the gemstone of my ring so that I can look at it and remember not to be hot-tempered; so that I won't get angry when I get wet in the rain or hear something I don't like; so that I won't rejoice at another person's unhappiness when I win against him; so that I will not want to destroy myself when someone accuses me of something I haven't done; so that I won't lose hope when I am not appreciated by others. In short, a bit of wisdom that will console me in every situation."

The preacher and the philosopher then said: "That's all very good, but finding such a word or phrase is not an easy job. The great and learned have uttered many such short phrases. Everyone knows some such thing and when it should be used. But if we want to find a single motto suitable for all occasions quickly, we must assemble all the wise and learned men of the city to a meeting. Each will be able to present the ideas he has found in books he has studied. Then you may select that word or phrase which you like."

"Let's do that," agreed the ruler. He ordered that letters be written to the learned and to the great orators of the time inviting them to the great assembly to be called "The Conference for the Review of Soothing Words."

*****

So the conference began. The most learned and best speakers of the time sat side by side, each talking in turn about patience, humility, restraint, and moderation. Poetry was recited; books and scriptures were cited.

But the ruler was still not satisfied. As each motto was proposed, he found something wrong with it. "This one is too brief, that one is too long. this one is silly, that one is awkward..."

On the final day of the conference, a villager wearing a felt cap happened enter the assembly bearing a message for the ruler. When he understood what all the commotion was about, he said:

"May I speak with your permission? I know something that is better than all the mottoes you have been proposing."

"If the members of the conference agree, you may speak."

But great scholar and orators of the age rose in opposition. "No, sir! What kind of a thing is this the governor proposes? All of us have turned the pages of many books. We have looked through the words of the great ones of the past, and we still haven't found a proper motto. And now an illiterate villager walks in to address this assembly!"

The villager bore all of this quietly. When they had finished ranting and railing against him, he lifted his hand for silence and said:

"All right, but you haven't yet found a suitable motto for the governor, so why not let me speak? I'm not going to eat anyone. If what I say is good, you may accept it; if not you can laugh at me."

"What he says is not bad," mused the governor.

"All right, " agreed the members of the conference. "If that is the your wish. We shall not oppose him. Let him speak!"

"As I understand it," said the man in the felt cap, "the governor wants a motto to inscribe on the gemstone of his ring. The words most restrain the reader and the listener from the evils of pride and disappointment. In my opinion, this can be found in four words. I don't know how to make it any fewer. On the gemstone of the ring these words should be inscribed: 'This too shall pass.'"

Upon hearing these words, the conference erupted in an uproar. Some said: "That is a worthless, stupid motto!"

Others shouted: "Such a motto will stop a man from working and struggling in life."

Others said: "Such a motto would be all right for the old days, but doesn't suit the present."

One after another the members criticized the motto as worthless, useless, old-fashioned, nonsense. . . .

But the ruler was stroking his beard thoughtfully as he listened to them.

"In my opinion," he said slowly, "the suggestion of the man in the felt cap is not bad at all. It is both short and soothing. When I recall that conditions are changeable, and that anger and happiness pass suddenly in life, I will find peace of mind. I will be able to take the time to pause and consider that I should not be either too sad or too proud. But I would like the conference to approve my choice."

But the members of the conference were not ready to accept the suggestion of the man in the felt cap. They looked at him angrily.

So the ruler announced: "Until something better can be found, these words will do."

He dismissed the assembly and summoned a jeweler to engrave with a diamond pen on the gemstone of his ring the words: "This too shall pass."

*****

This story was also told by the 19th century poet Asrar Sabzevari in these verses:

> A king had a valuable pearl to set in a ring;
> All of his rings had gemstones.
> He wanted an inscription with a double meaning
> (To remind him) whenever he looked at it:
> That he not be negligent when he was rejoicing,
> That he not suffer unduly when he sorrowed.
> He approached the wise of his age,
> But found their suggestions unsatisfying;
> At that juncture, a dervish appeared
> And said: "Write these words: 'This Too Shall Pass.'"

15
THE MADMAN RIDING A CANE

One day some people in a certain town saw a man riding a bamboo cane. He held the cane with one hand while he brandished a whip with the other. Like a man riding a horse, he ran and jumped around the field. All the time he was laughing and having fun. From time to time he would strike his 'horse' with the whip and urge his steed to even greater speeds. He paid no attention the people gaping at him as he ran about. Children gathered around him and pointed him out to each other, saying, "He's crazy! He's mad!"

People remembered seeing this man before walking around in the streets, but talking to no one. He had kept his head lowered and looking straight ahead. People thought he was just some ordinary person, but this day they realized that the poor fellow was indeed mad.

After the man had thus run around the field several times and while he was still busy doing so, an old man passing by stopped and called out to him:

"Do you have any idea what you are doing?" the old man cried.

"Of course I do," answered the man with a broad smile.

"Can't you see I'm riding my horse?"

"Horse?" demanded the old man. "What horse? That isn't a horse! It's a bamboo cane!"

"What's that to you whether it's a stick or a horse? Is what I am doing costing you anything?"

"No," said the old man shaking his head. "It's nothing to me. If it were, I would go to the authorities and complain about you. But, really, sir, what you're doing is senseless. You're making a fool of yourself. It's madness. Someone right in his head would never do such a thing. I just wanted to point that out to you."

The madman stopped in front of the old man. "Tell me, what does someone right in his head do that is not foolish and is reasonable?"

"That's obvious. He does his duty. He does work, useful work. He earns and manages his affairs and life. At times he rests, at times he worships God, he studies, . . . things like that."

"Very good!" said the madman. "A sane person takes care of his work, his life, his house, his worship, his sleep, his reading, his duties, everything. But doesn't he have the right to take the air for pleasure, to play in the playground, to laugh, to busy himself with some hobby. In short, doesn't he have the right to relax and enjoy himself?"

"Certainly," said the old man. "When a person has finished what has to be done, that person can relax and have a little fun: sports, for example, or chess, painting, games, taking the air, and a thousand other things, but they must not cause anyone any trouble and they must be reasonable."

"Reasonable!" echoed the madman. "Look, if some one

enjoys horseback riding and does it in a place that causes no trouble to anyone else, and if while riding he laughs and rejoices, is there something wrong in that?"

"Of course not," said the other. "There's nothing wrong in that! Horseback riding is both a kind of exercise and a source of pleasure. But riding a horse is different from riding a cane!"

"How is it different?" asked the madman.

"Ah!" groaned the old man. "Why do you make everything so difficult for me? Is there no difference between riding a horse and riding a stick? What are you saying? Are you crazy?"

"I am not crazy!" retorted the madman. In my opinion there is no difference between riding a horse and riding a bamboo cane. I know that I wouldn't be any happier riding a horse than I am now! Are you so mean-spirited that you don't want to see me enjoy myself?"

"Certainly not!" protested the other. "Be as happy as you please, but why are you riding a cane instead of a horse? People will think you are crazy."

"Well, by God, I am not to blame," said the madman. "People who think I'm crazy have horses or don't like to ride horses. By making fun of me they want to make others think they are very smart.

"But I know that though I want to ride a horse, I don't have one, so I am making do with this piece of bamboo! There is no harm in it to anyone. If I were riding on your roof, you could complain about it, but this is a public field. I am enjoying myself and those who are watching me are enjoying themselves too, more so than if they were watching me ride a horse! There is no reason for me to mope about because I don't have a horse. I have done my work and taken care of my other duties. Now I am having some fun for half an hour. I like to ride horses and today this cane is my horse.

"The madman is he who eats his own bread and then takes the trouble to keep me from enjoying myself! If you have something more sensible to do, go do it so that you don't become crazy!"

Having said this, the madman resumed running, jumping, laughing, and enjoying himself around the field.

The other man shook his head, saying to himself: "The poor fellow is mad!"

But which of the two was really mad?

16

THE LOVESICK BEGGAR

In a certain city, the ruler had a daughter who excelled all other girls in beauty. Naturally, as a result many of the young men of the city were suitors for her hand. Some of these young men even claimed that they were in love with her. They were lovesick.

What does being in love mean? Well, being in love means that some one loves something or someone very much and is willing to make great sacrifices to get what he or she wants.

There are people who like books and who try to read as many books as they can. But there are others who are prepared to forgo good clothing, who eat less and abstain from other things in order to save more money to buy books. These people may be called book and reading lovers. They are willing to sacrifice anything in order to get their hands on books.

Friendship is one thing, but love is more and includes sacrifice. For example a man wants to marry a certain girl, but if the girl and her family do not accept him, he may go off and look for another girl.

But there is another person who will accept difficult conditions to marry. He will wait long years and will

ignore everything except what his heart is set on. If he cannot marry the girl of his choice, he will not marry another and remain single. That is one whom he call 'lovesick.'

Such love is near madness and, fortunately, not frequent in this day and age. It was more common in the past.

So this passion is a flame that rejection and coldness on the part of the beloved will not kill. If a lover has a sound mind and body, he will try to impress with his faithfulness and demonstrate that he is loyal and worthy of the affection of his beloved. But if he is not sound of mind, he may do things which disgrace himself and his family, and even harm others. Such a person is sick or mad.

Be that as it may, this ruler's daughter had a flock of suitors seeking her hand in marriage. Some of these claimed that they were deeply in love with her. They were busy thinking about how to make a suitable place for married life and to ask for her hand.

Among these young men there was also a beggar who roamed the streets begging from people. One day he saw the ruler's daughter in the street and the sight of her filled his heart with light. He fell head over heels in love with her. "If there is happiness in this world," he said to himself, "it will be found with her."

He followed the girl to her home in order to know where she lived. After that he could not leave that street. The poor man was lovesick. He had fallen in love and with the daughter of the most powerful man in the city! A beggar was hardly suitable to be her husband, but he didn't think about that.

So the beggar became the beggar in the ruler's street. He tried to meet the girl to learn how she felt about him.

From dawn to dusk he walked about that street. Whenever the girl appeared he would stand still and stare at her longingly, forgetting himself completely. Again and again he searched his mind for some excuse to speak with her, but he was afraid.

Things were thus until one day the ruler's daughter happened to notice him. Feeling sorry for the beggar, she smiled at him.

The unfortunate beggar, seeing that smile, thought that it meant she had feelings for him and had accepted his love. It did not occur to him that such a girl was far above him and impossible to reach.

The young beggar's hopes grew greater and he became even more lovesick and, perhaps, a little crazier. Now he always hung around the house of the ruler, he made the area his home as soon as he had gotten the money for his daily food from begging. He always watched the house in the hope of seeing the girl he loved, and prayed that he would be able to wed her some day. But after a time, the girl no longer paid him any mind. The beggar decided this indifference was really bashfulness!

When a person is lost in his own feelings and desires, he pays no attention to the reality around him. He does not realize that others see things and understand them. Gradually the people of the street learned the reason for the beggar's constant presence in their neighborhood. After a short time there was no one who did not know the beggar's secret:

There are many sharp eyes in this world,
They see what everyone else is doing.

One thing that people like to do is to see what others are doing and talk about their affairs. The beggar's love was becoming a public scandal!

The rulers daughter heard about it, too. As it happened, she was an intelligent girl. She knew that if she concealed the matter from her parents, she would regret it. So one day she told them about the lovesick beggar in their street.

The ruler angrily gave orders that the beggar be warned to stay away from that street. But the beggar believed in the power of his love and was not able to tear himself away from that house. From time to time he returned there and recited poetry or wrote love letters to the girl.

Learning this, the ruler told his retainers: "If I see him around here one more time, I'll do something to him that will cause him to lose his head, literally!"

But the ruler's daughter felt sorry for the beggar and sent a message to him: "What is this hope you have which is impossible to fulfill? There is something brewing now that if you come here again you will put your life in danger. Do not come here again or you will be sorry."

The lovesick beggar replied to the messenger: "Whatever bad happens to me, let it happen! I shall sacrifice my head, my life, and my existence for my love. They can do nothing more than beat me and torture me! From the day I saw her smile, I have no fear of anyone."

When the girl heard this she decided that she would have to act to save the young man. She sent the messenger to bring the beggar to her.

He came and stood before her humbly. He was in the presence of the idol of his dreams.

"What do you want?" she asked him. "You are disturbing us and putting yourself in danger."

"This is what I want," said the lover fearlessly. "I shall surrender life and soul in the way of love. When you smiled at me, why did you not speak to me? If you are my friend, let come what may. I am in love and I fear no one. I am willing to sacrifice myself for my love!"

"But you do not know the meaning of love," said the girl. "Getting killed or love-madness is not sacrifice in the way of love! Love is not death, love is living. A long time has passed since that smile. If you really loved me, you would have done something to make yourself suitable for marriage with me. But you are still a beggar! Sacrifice would have been to stop being lazy and begging for your living. You would want to make yourself into some one whose love I would be proud to accept. If you had least bit of intelligence, you would know that life is not a game and that we are not suited to each other."

"But," protested the beggar, "why did you smile at me that day and drive me mad?"

"A sane man does not go mad for a smile," said the girl. "That smile was fire, and with fire food may be cooked or a house burned down. If you had been wise, that fire would have perfected you, but you have allowed it to destroy you. Do you understand your mistake?"

"You deceived me!" cried the beggar. "You led me astray!"

"I did not deceive you," she replied. "Each person must know his own place. That day I laughed at your foolishness and stupidity. It was not the smile of love. I was laughing at you. I don't want to be the wife of a beggar! I wanted to make you think about your life and to change it so that you would gain respect and honor.

"But you deceived yourself and called your foolish hopes love! Love is something which builds and constructs. What kind of a love is it that causes sorrow and ruins one?"

The beggar fell into thought. His head was bowed in shame. After a few moments, he said:

"You speak the truth. You are right. I have deceived myself. My love was not true love; it was madness. I've come to my senses now."

And in fact he had come to his senses. It was late, but it had happened. After that, the beggar was no longer seen in the vicinity of the ruler's house. He went away and made himself worthy of respect by working hard. The following year he married a girl suitable to his new status and raised children who did them honor.

Love had replaced love-madness.

17

FRESH WATER, DIFFERENT WATER

Once there was a man named Ahmad who earned his living by carrying water to the thirsty. Every morning he would throw his waterskin over his shoulder and go to the spring to fill it. Then he would carry the water through the city streets. People would drink from the small cup he had with him and then give him a few pennies for the water.

One day as he was walking through the streets after having filled his waterskin, he met another water-carrier coming from the opposite direction.

Ahmad called the other man and said: "Let me drink a little of your water."

The other looked at Ahmad in surprise. "Are you crazy? You're a water-carrier and you have water. Pour a little out and drink it!"

"That's true," said Ahmad, "I have water, but I'm tired of drinking this water. I want to taste some different water now. Different water will have a different delight!"

"And just where are you coming from?" demanded the other water-carrier, "and where are you taking that water?"

"I'm coming from the spring," replied Ahmad, "and I taking this load to headman's kitchen."

"Well, you're wrong," said the other. "Just because something is different, it doesn't mean that it is better. It would have a better taste if you didn't have any and needed it. You aren't really tired of the water, you probably don't realize its taste. Perhaps that cup you drink it from isn't clean. Perhaps you're hungry. Perhaps you're lazy. Perhaps you're tired of working as a water-carrier and you're looking for some excuse to get out of it.

"But you aren't thirsty!" the other continued. "In my opinion a person who has spring water in his waterskin and asks others for water doesn't know the value of water at all! You're just playing around at being thirsty."

"What are you saying?" protested Ahmad. "Everybody enjoys something different. People don't eat just one kind of food. A person who usually eats stew sometimes eats rice pilaf. Someone who usually eats pilaf occasionally eats stew!"

"Stew and pilaf are two different dishes and people eat one or the other for variety," retorted the other water-carrier. "But water is water! The water in my waterskin is not sherbet; it's just plain water. It isn't more fluid or wetter, but it is the water that suits me and my work. You're behaving as though you don't have confidence in yourself. You're like those who think that whatever someone else has is better than what they have. Every day it is something else! They are embarrassed to be themselves! Yes, a change of water and weather is pleasant, but novelty and newness will not cure your problems!"

"Just listen to yourself!" cried Ahmad. "I just asked you for some water, not a lesson in philosophy!"

"I feel sorry for you," said the other. "You have a problem but don't know what it is. You're not thirsty. Thirst leads a person to water. You have water and yet you complain about being thirsty! Look, when you pour water into that cup, does your arm hurt?"

"Yes, yes!" said Ahmad. "My arm hurts a lot. Every time I raise it to pour water it bothers me a lot. It's very painful!"

"Didn't I tell you?" demanded the other. "So it's plain that you are really thirsty but can't pour the water! The reason why you think you want to taste the different water in my waterskin is, in truth, the pain in your arm. You should go to a doctor and have him look at your arm. A sick person is always looking for excuses and thinks that others are the cause of his trouble. Eggs should be cubes and parallel lines should meet!"

"Well, it's true that there is nothing wrong with the water," said Ahmad with a sigh, "but I feel tired and listless. Now, will you give me a cup of water or not?"

The other water-carrier filled his cup and handed it to Ahmad. Ahmad drank it and said: "Despite everything you said, this water is sweeter and very tasty!"

"It's just as I said," insisted the other. "If you have your arm treated by a doctor, you won't feel this way any more. You enjoy the water I carry because you are tired of carrying water and blame it. You imagine that the water in my waterskin has a better taste, even though you are taking water from the spring to the house of headman.

"But, friend, the water I am carrying came from the pool in the courtyard of the headman's house! I am taking it to give to his sheep and cattle! It's the same water that you get from the spring!"

"Then you are a bad person for not telling me that in the first place," said Ahmad.

The other water-carrier shook his head and smiled sadly.

"Now that I've told you say such a thing!" he said. "If I hadn't, you'd be going on about how good it was. Up to now you were complaining about the spring water, now you are complaining about me! A tired and sick person is always complaining. There was nothing wrong with the spring water, if you say there was, you don't know good water and aren't worthy to be a water-carrier! Go on your way and thank God Most High for what you He has put in your hands!"

18
THE DEVIL BE CURSED!

One day during the time of the Prophet Daniel, a man came to him and said: "O Daniel! Save me from the devil!"

"What has the devil done?" asked Daniel.

"Nothing," said the man. "On one side you prophets and saints teach us religion and ethics, while on the other side Satan won't let us be good! He won't let us do good deeds. He won't let us stay away from bad things."

"How does he stop you?" asked Daniel. "Does he bring an army against you? Does he do battle with you and force you to do bad things?"

"Not like that," said the man, "but he is always tempting us. He makes bad things look attractive to our eyes. He tricks us night and day and he won't let us be honest and righteous."

"You have to explain further what Satan does," said Daniel. "Look, does he, for example, tickle you when you are performing your prayers and prevent you from praying? When you want to give some money to charity, does he seize your wrist and stop you? When you want to go to the mosque, does he throw a rope around your neck and drag you to a gamblers' den? When you want to say something good to people, does he go into your mouth and say bad things to them on your behalf? When you are conducting business, does he make you cheat them? Does he do any of these things?"

"No," said the man touching his beard. "He can't do things like that. But, by God, I don't know how to tell you how he interferes in everything I do. He does it in such a way that before I know it he's done some dirty deed and gone off! I'm helpless against him. He is responsible for all of my sins."

"I'm surprised that you complain so much about the devil," said the prophet. "Tell me, my good man, how is that he cannot trick me? Why can't he ever deceive me? I don't have horns and a tail; I'm just like you. Maybe you aren't being fair to blame him for all of your sins."

"No," said the man shaking his head. "I've tried very hard to be a good man, but the devil is my enemy and won't let me be good."

"That's very strange!" said Daniel. "Where do you live?"

"Nearby," the man replied. "In this area. Thanks to the devil, the people here don't think that I'm a good person. I don't know what to do."

"What is your name?" asked Daniel.

"My name is Hasan-Ali-Jafar."

"How wonderful! So you are Hasan-Ali-Jafar!"

"What about it?" asked Hasan-Ali-Jafar in surprise. "Have you heard anything about me?"

"I hadn't heard anything about you until today," said Daniel. "As it happens, Satan came to me today and complained about you! He said: 'Save me from Hasan-Ali-Jafar.'"

"The devil asked you to protect him from me?" cried the

man. "What was his complaint?"

"He said that he couldn't do anything with Hasan-Ali-Jafar," replied the prophet Daniel. "He said that you were always bothering him. He said that you had been very unfair to him. Then he asked me to find you and advise you to leave him alone!"

"So," said the man. "Didn't you ask him what I had done to him?"

Daniel said:

"I asked that very thing. 'What has Hasan-Ali-Jafar done?' Satan answered: 'Nothing, but I am the devil and I am cursed by God. On the first day I got permission from God to come to this world and God established certain limits for my activities. Our agreement was that all evil deeds would be under my control, and good deeds under the control of the believers.

"'But this Hasan-Ali-Jafar constantly interferes in my work. He's trying to step into my shoes! And then he blames and curses me! For example, he could pray, but he doesn't. He could fast, but he doesn't. He could give money to charity, but he doesn't. He does a hundred evil things that he doesn't have to, and then he blames me for them!

"'Wine belongs to me and he goes and drinks it. Double-dealing and chicanery are my specialties, he excels at them. The mosque is God's house, but the tavern and the gambling den are mine. Instead of going to the mosque, he is always in my houses. Coarse speech and bad behavior are in my province, but he is skilled in them.

"'What can I say? This Hasan-Ali-Jafar is always tricking me, but whenever he gets into a difficulty he curses me! When he does business with people and cheats them and puts their money in his deep pockets, he accuses me.

When did I ever take him by the hand and force him to enter a bad place? When did I ever push food down his throat and break his fast? I don't know, O Daniel, what I have done to him that he causes so many problems for me. Why doesn't he leave me alone? I beg you, you always talk to the people and give them good counsel. Summon this Hasan-Ali-Jafar and tell him to leave me alone!'"

"So," continued Daniel, "you see that Satan had many causes for complaint about you. I was looking for you to tell you to stop trying to take his place. Well, when you interfere in the devil's work, he has a right to interfere in yours and make things bad for you.

"You say that Satan never forced you to do anything, he just tempts you. If that is so, don't listen to him! Try to keep to good speech and deeds. Then you will become like me and you won't have any more complaints about the devil, nor will he have any about you!

"When you do something wrong, and then curse Satan, he has the right to complain about you. You must be so good that he will not be able to curse you."

Upon hearing these words of Daniel, Hasan-Ali-Jafar became very ashamed of himself and said:

"You are right. It was all my own fault that I did the work of the devil. I must change myself, if not, Satan will not take responsibility for what I do, may he be cursed!"

19

THE SNAKE AND THE SNAKE CATCHER

O nce there was a snake catcher who was very good at his work and had a lot of experience. He would place traps baited with a pleasant-smelling paste by snake holes and then recite some strange spells and incantations over the trap. That done, he would take his dagger in his hand and wait patiently for the snake to come out of its hole. If the snake went into the trap, he would catch it and take it to town to sell to a medicine factory or a zoo. If the snake were too big to fit in his trap, he would kill it and sell the skin.

One day while he was walking in the desert, the snake catcher saw a large snake with beautiful markings on its skin. He followed the snake in order to learn where it lived. Then he put the aromatic paste in a box by the entrance to the snake's nest so that when the snake came out, attracted by the scent of the paste, it would go into the box.

The snake catcher sat down and waited a long time, but the snake did not appear. The man added to the paste and changed it several times, but still the snake did not come out.

"Maybe he doesn't like the smell of this paste," thought the snake catcher. "Perhaps he would prefer a different paste."

He prepared a different paste again and again;
He recited different spells over and over.

But the snake was not in its underground nest! Its home had two entrances and it had gone out the other entrance. Protected from sight by a hill, it lay curled up basking in the warm sunlight. It said to itself: "Let the snake catcher wait there and recite spells until he gets tired of it."

As it happened, Jesus was walking along that very path and greeted the snake catcher and smiled.

The snake catcher answered the greeting and Jesus walked on. When he reached the top of a small hill, the snake saw him and greeted him, and said:

"O Jesus, do you see how foolish humans are? I have the experience of the three hundred years of my life and that thirty-year old man is sitting in front of the entrance of my home with a trap and some scented paste. He thinks that with a trick he can lure me out of the hole and catch me in his trap. Believe me, if he did not have that dagger in his hand, I'd go and teach him a lesson about snake catching!"

Jesus laughed and said: "Well, everyone has some sort of job. He enjoys what he is doing, but you be careful and watch out for yourself!"

And Jesus left the snake and continued on his path and did what he had set out to do. An hour or two later he happened to return on the very same path. When he reached the place where the snake had been, he saw that it wasn't

there. A little further on he saw the snake catcher with a bulging bag on his shoulders getting ready to leave.

"So," asked Jesus the man, "what happened?"

"I caught the snake," he man said. "It's in my box."

Jesus approached the box and saw the snake peering out of a small opening in it. Jesus asked the snake:

"With all you centuries of experience and bragging, you were finally caught! I can't do anything for you because snake catching is not a sin and I have no right to rebuke him. But you knew about the paste and the trap!"

"O Jesus!" said the snake. "I know the scent of every kind of paste and I know the shape of every kind of trap. The snake catcher didn't catch me with the paste or trap."

"Then how did he catch you?"

"When he realized that I would not fall into his trap or try to get the paste," sighed the snake, "he changed his plan, but I didn't know it!"

"What happened?" asked Jesus.

"I went into my hole to sleep. After a while I heard the sound of prayers. The snake catcher had put aside the paste and spread some green brush at the entrance of my home. He hid the trap behind that and began to recite incantations. In those incantations I heard the Name of God frequently and he spoke of water, greenery, happiness, delight, purity, and faith. I thought that the snake catcher had gone away and someone similar to a prophet like yourself had taken his place. For that reason, my heart brimming with purity and friendship, I came out and fell into the trap and was caught! Believe me, I have never heard of this trick as long as I have been a snake."

"Yes," said Jesus reflectively, "there are all kinds in this world. Many tricksters speak of justice in order to achieve their unjust ends. They clothe their deceptions with the Name of God, too. One must be watchful and be sure the godly person is what he says he is."

Then Jesus looked at the snake and said: "If I buy you from the snake catcher and set you free, will you swear never to bother people or bite them again?"

The snake shook its head. "No, I cannot swear such a thing. It is against my nature. I'm supposed to bite. In any case, even if I weren't tricked again, I would eventually die in my nest. Now that I have been caught with the Name of God, it is better that I be of some use to mankind. Perhaps God will forgive my sins."

"Yes," said Jesus. "A snake's poison can hurt and even kill people. But a wise man may buy that poison and make a useful medicine out of it, and that is better."

20
THE MILLSTONE

Shaykh Abu Said was a wise and learned dervish who had established his hospice (*khaneqah*, house of dervishes) in Nishabur and had many students and disciples.

One day, as the shaykh and a group of his disciples and friends were passing across the countryside, they came upon a mill. It was powered by the water of a spring which flowed into the mill's flue and turned the millstone to grind wheat and barley into flour.

Now, a mill has two stones. The bottom stone does not move, but the upper stone turns on it and grinds the kernels of wheat and barley into flour which pours out of a hole between the two stones. As the upper stone turns and grinds the flour is caught in a special container.

When Abu Said got near the mill, he told the others to wait a few moments while he went in to look at the mill. "I'll be back shortly," he promised.

Inside the mill there was a miller and his apprentice. There were also some villagers who had brought their wheat and barley to be ground and were waiting their turns. The shaykh, in his dervish robes, entered the mill and greeted them with "Peace be upon you!" Then he stood to one side to watch.

The grain of one of the villagers had just been ground. He poured the flour into some sacks and left. The grain of the next man was poured into the mill and his was ground. He collected his flour and went in the same way. More people came in carrying loads of grain to be ground. Abu Said remained standing at one side, not taking his eyes off the mill. One of the men noticed that Abu Said was watching the turning of the millstone as though he could not get enough of it. The man went to the miller and whispered: "Look at that dervish! You'd think he's never seen a mill!"

"It's not that," said the miller to his customer. "I know those people. They reflect about everything. They make something out of it. Forget about him, let him watch as long as he wants to."

Another said in alarm: "But, see! This believer is weeping! Look at his eyes! Perhaps he thinks the turning of the stone is a miracle and is remembering God." Another said: "No, brother, he's a dervish and a beggar. He's waiting for some one to give him a handful of flour." But Abu Said paid no attention to the whisperings about him. From his own thoughts, tears were filling his eyes and rolling down his cheeks. And he continued to stand and watch for a while.

When a considerable time had passed and the shaykh had not come out of the mill, his companions went in and stood around him inside the mill. One of them said to Abu Said: "It would appear that the good shaykh likes to watch the mill work."

The miller's customers were all ears waiting to hear the shaykh's reply. The shaykh replied in measured tones. "It is not a matter of liking or disliking the mill," he said.

"But I like the advice of the millstone very much. It is talking to me and giving me wisdom. Do you know what the stone is saying?"

"You know best," replied the disciple.

"This stone is speaking with the voice of inspiration," said Abu Said. "It is saying: 'You call yourself a dervish and you are pleased by the thought that you are wise-hearted and aware. You go about the world and make sense of it and you think that this is work.

"'But it is I who am wise-hearted and aware. I cannot go anywhere, even with that I move more than you do and my movements have a greater benefit for others.

"'You think that you wear coarse clothing and that that is the sign of your righteousness, but I am better than you, for I take coarse grain and turn it into soft flour.

"'You think that you must travel the world and then learn that few people know truth and all are bewildered, but despite this bewilderment, I know truth.

"'You think that because you don't know everything you must make a profession of wandering and speak ill of the world, but I am better than you, for I perform my duty in accordance with my skill and ability and I do not bother others.

"'You think that a person who has grown old in a mill has no experience of the world, but I know that many beards grow white in time, but their owners know less of life than does this miller.

"'You think you are free of the world, yet you take things from people and return nothing, but though I am just a millstone and have not pretensions, I return everything I take from people after making it twice as good and I keep nothing for myself. . . .'"

Abu Said looked at his companions and continued: "I am afire with the words spoken by this millstone and see that it spoke correctly. We are nothing but claims and pretensions, but the stone is a doer. We are nothing but talk, while it is real. We are idle, but it works. We are searching, but it has found. We are on the way, but it has arrived."

Abu Said's face was wet with tears and his companions were deeply affected by this. But the customers stared at the dervish and his followers, not understanding what he was saying. One of them said to the miller: "Do you understand what he was driving at?"

The miller nodded his as he worked. "I understand. That's what these people are always doing. They're a bunch of enlightened dervishes. They talk about everything they come across. They talk well and have good taste. They try to find a mystery in everything. They speak in parables, they weep, and they laugh. They advise and counsel people. Sometimes they are right, sometimes that they are wrong.

"But the reins are in our hands, brother! It is we who turn the wheat and barley into flour and enable people to live. There are a lot of good people in this world, but it is we workers who make the world turn."

21
GOOD FORTUNE AND MISFORTUNE

One day Anushirvan, an ancient king of Persia, famous for his justice and wisdom, who reigned for nearly half a century and died three years after the birth of the Prophet Muhammad (ﷺ), left his palace with his entourage to go hunting. The hunting party came upon some ruins far from any habitation. Anushirvan rode over to the ruins to see what the place was like and why it was in ruins. A royal guard followed him at a little distance.

The king saw a miserable man behind one of the broken walls. He had a brick for a pillow and a jug of water at his side.

He was talking to himself. He was saying: "What kind of justice is this? What kind of a country is this in which I can be so unfortunate? And they say Anushirvan is just! I thank God, but this is no kind of a life! This is not justice! This..."

Anushirvan stood before the man and asked him: "What are you doing here?"

Seeing the stranger in his splendid dress, the unfortunate man was frightened.

"Nothing," he replied. "I don't have anything to do with

anyone. "This land is desert, it doesn't belong to anyone. The desert belongs to God."

"No," said Anushirvan. "I heard you talking and complaining. Who has done an injustice to you?"

"I don't know," answered the poor man. "There wasn't anyone here to complain to, but my life is very hard."

"I heard you mention the name of Anushirvan," said the king. "Do you have any complaint about him?"

The poor man thought: "Perhaps this is Anushirvan himself! What an opportunity if it is he! I'll tell him my story, come what may."

So the man rose in respect and then sat down again. He said: "Are you King Anushirvan the Just?"

"Yes," replied the king. "I am Anushirvan. People call me the just."

"In my opinion," said the poor man, "whoever calls you just should have his mouth stuffed with dirt, because he is lying! Is it justice that I beg for thirty long years in the country of Anushirvan and get no reward from life? My clothes are worn out and my house is a ruin. My stomach is empty, yet you are my king and you are called just!

"You are so happy and I without anything
And yet you say 'I am just!'"

King Anushirvan decided that the wretched man was very upset to take such liberties in his speech with his king. The king tried to comfort him, saying: "It is true that you appear to be very unfortunate. You are right, but I didn't know anything about your plight until now. Can we forget the past and let me send you to a hospital to be treated?"

"I'm not sick," said the poor man. "I don't need to go to a hospital. My problem is misfortune and poverty."

"Very well," said the king. "I am pleased that you speak the truth so plainly. Bad fortune is not cured with medicine, it is cured with good fortune. That is something that all people search for. The affairs of the world are based upon that search. If people do not work to improve their lives, there won't be anything left in the world and the world will become a desert. But, tell me, what have you been doing in your search for a better life?"

"What have I been doing? I've traveled all over this land for thirty years. Wherever I knocked on a door, it has been shut on me. What can I do? The rest should be asked of you who are King Anushirvan the Just."

"All right," said the king, "if I am asked I shall answer that you have a right to prosper. Of course, all people are not the same. Everyone cannot be very learned, rich, and powerful. Yet everyone has a right to his portion in life and to peace, and so do you. Now I shall order that we learn who has your portion. They will give you what they owe you."

"But no one whom I know owes me anything," protested the poor man. "What I'm saying is that if you are just I should get my just dues."

"So," said the king, "if no one owes you anything, do you know who has stolen that which is your right? Have I taken it?"

"No, you haven't taken anything from me, but there is so much affluence and comfort in life. Where is mine?"

The king looked into the poor man's eyes.

"It is everywhere. But it is like this: if you are thirsty, don't you have to extend your arm and take the water jug and drink from it? Life is like that. If you want to make your life better, you have to get busy yourself and go after it."

"If I reach out, they'll call me a thief!" retorted the unfortunate man. "Or they'll say that I'm a beggar and they won't let me get anything."

"I'm not suggesting that you try to take or beg things from others," said the king. "What I mean that just as you must make an effort to lift the water jug in order to get your drink of water, so you must make your own efforts to improve your life. You have to agree that thirty years of wandering and begging has not made you rich or happy. You have to try another way to save yourself from poverty and more complaining about your life."

"That's right," said the poor man, "I should do something else, but I don't have any other skill."

"Good," said the king. "Now tell me, has Anushirvan taken your job away from you?"

"No," said the other. "I didn't have a job for you to take. I don't know what I want to say."

"I know what you want to say," said Anushirvan. "You want good clothes. You want good food. You want a good home. You want a wife, children, honor, and respect. If you cannot be, for example, a royal minister, you want to be like other people who had quiet, prosperous lives."

"Yes, that's it!" exclaimed the man. "That's what I want. I have such things, I wouldn't have any complaints about the king!"

"Yes, anyone who had such things would not be sleeping in these ruins. Everyone must work or no one will have anything and I would not have a kingdom to govern."

"But who will give me work?" asked the unfortunate

man.

"A good question!" said the king. "Now that I know you I shall give you a job, a good job, an honorable job, but only if you yourself want it. Are you prepared to come tomorrow and take the place of my grand vizier Buzurgmehr and do what he does? You will have his responsibilities, his power, and his respect."

"No," said the poor man. "I do not possess the knowledge and wisdom of Buzurgmehr. I can't do his job. As soon as they find out that I don't have his skill, you will criticize me and others will also, and my life will be disgraced."

"All right," said the king. "If you can't or don't want to take the place of Buzurgmehr, would you like to come with me today and take the place of the chief huntsman? You would organize the hunt and I'll appoint him to some other position. You will receive his salary and all the privileges that go with the job."

"No," said the poor man. "What do I know about leading a hunt? I know nothing about organizing a hunt. If I were to take the job, no one would obey me and everything will fall apart."

"So that's not suitable for you either?" Anushirvan said. "Look, I'm ready to give you an important job, but you won't accept one! Perhaps you accept a less important job. Would you agree to work in my library with the other librarians and scholars?"

"No," said the poor man. "I can 't read and write. What can I do with books?"

"How odd!" said the king. "You mean you have been traveling about this country for thirty years and haven't even learned the alphabet? Dear friend, you could have learned that in three months! If you had spent one hour a week during those years in a library, you could have prepared yourself for some profession better than begging! But it's not too late!. I'm not trying to blame you. You can still learn. I want to wake you up!"

"I'm wide awake!" cried the unfortunate man. "I know a hundred illiterates who have millions!"

"That' so," said the king, "but none of them have taken refuge in ruins and complain of lack of work. They didn't get their money from my treasury. They worked and earned what they have with effort, brains, and ambition."

"Or they inherited it," smirked the poor man.

"You are complaining about Anushirvan," said Anushirvan. "An inheritance would be their father's property. Anyway, if you know hundreds that inherited their money, I know thousands who worked for theirs. All right, now tell me, what is my shortcoming in your affairs?"

"You should have done something to make me happy," insisted the poor man.

"That's not the way things are," said Anushirvan. "You have already answered your own complaints when you say you know many illiterates who have millions. If the responsibility for your misfortune is mine, then I may say that I have ruled so that a hundred illiterates have made their fortunes. They consider me just. If the responsibility is not mine, then what have I to do with your good or bad fortune?"

The king continued patiently: "You have already refused the jobs I have offered you, but you haven't told me what you want me to do. Should I order the treasury to give you a thousand pieces of silver?"

"That wouldn't be a bad idea!" grinned the poor man.

"As it happens, it would be a very bad idea," said

Anushirvan. "The money in the treasury is not my money, it belongs to the people and the kingdom. If I gave their money to you, the people would no longer say that I am Anushirvan the Just."

"Yes," said the poor men thoughtfully. "Then they would call you Anushirvan the Tyrant. Well, then, what should I do?"

"Now that you ask that question, you're coming to your senses. Let's see, what should be done in your case? You have come to realize your situation a little late in life. You should have been thinking about learning some trade when you were much younger. It doesn't matter what. Any good trade would do for you. If you had learned to be a carpenter, a blacksmith, a tailor, a mason, a farmer, or any of a thousand other trades, you be a master at it now. If you had studied something during these thirty years instead of wandering aimlessly, you might be a scholar now. If, instead of sleeping in these ruins today, you had gotten up and done something useful such as weeping a street, you would begin to regain your self-respect. You would begin to drive away misfortune and open the door of good fortune.

"But instead you lie here and complain of Anushirvan! That won't help anything. Isn't that right?"

The unfortunate man stood up and stood respectfully as he answered his king.

"You speak the truth, your majesty. I understand now that I have neglected my own duty to myself and the world. This very day I shall go and start to work in something. There are a thousand things I can do. I have been flying from work, but there is something else I want to know. What does this justice of Anushirvan mean?"

"It means," said the king, "that I take care that people

do not act unjustly to themselves. That they not steal or abuse the rights of others. That no one goes over the wall of another. That the people pay attention to their own affairs and be hopeful for a better future. That they benefit from their own labor and abilities.

"It means that I try to the best of my ability to involve the people in my work so that it be fair and honest. If people call me just, perhaps it is for these things. If you learn a trade and do your work honesty, you too will be called just."

"That's true," said the man. "Now I want to work and study. Since I am in the presence of Anushirvan the Just, let him do something to make my journey shorter."

Anushirvan called the guard and said: "Take this unfortunate man and give him clothing, a place to stay, and whatever work he can do. If he can be fortunate in life, let him be so!"

So the man who had complained of his bad fortune and knew no trade was given a place as apprentice to an blacksmith. When he applied himself, he was sharp, alert, and learned quickly. A year later he was accepted as a partner by his master and a few years later he was able to open his own shop.

Over the entrance of his workshop he placed a sign. On it was written: "Anushirvan the Just Workshop."